Poverty Informed Practice IN EDUCATION

10 Actions to Try Now!

CHAD DULL, Ed.D.
POVERTY INFORMED PRACTICE, LLC

Foreword by Dr. Sara Goldrick-Rab

Design and layout of book and cover by Monica Durr
Illustrations by Matthew Bergs

This book can be available to audiences as part of a speaking engagement package.
Learn more at: povertyinformedpractice.com

First Edition

Published by
Poverty Informed Practice, LLC
La Crosse, WI 54601

Orders: (608) 799-0782, cddull@charter.net
www.povertyinformedpractice.com

Design and layout of book and cover by Monica Durr
Illustrations by Matthew Bergs
Printed and bound in United States of America

Library of Congress Cataloging-in-Publication Data

ISBN

To my mom and dad who were broke, but not broken, and taught me if you can help, you should.

Acknowledgments

I would like to acknowledge and thank several people who have helped make my dream of a book into reality. First, my children, Hannah and Cameron, who have had to listen to me rant about unfairness and injustice their entire lives. I used to say "I wish they knew what I knew without living what I've lived," but I see them as young adults making a difference in the world, and I realize they know more than I ever could have dreamt. I'm so proud of them both. Dr. Denise Vujnovich, the best boss I ever had, for allowing me to learn and grow and form a point of view about education under the umbrella of safety and support she created. Dr. Donna Beegle gave me training and friendship and made me believe you could make a difference speaking and writing. Dr. Sara Goldrick-Rab was always kind, inspirational, and supportive, even when I was just a Twitter follower. I cannot express the depth of my gratitude for her support in writing the foreword for this book. Dr. Russell Lowery-Hart showed me you can lead from a place of love and succeed. My mom, Dawn Simonson, believed in me even when there was no evidence to support that choice. My dad, Greg Dull, who gave me my love for underdogs. My good friend, Josiah Litant, who said to me the first time he heard me speak about poverty, "you should just do this for a living."

I also want to thank my editor Catherine Tyink. Her ability to distill my passionate ramblings and stories into a meaningful and coherent narrative has been a true gift. Without her, I would still be looking at five years of essays and trying to figure out how it could be a book.

Finally, I need to thank my partner in this work, Mandy Church. None of this happens without our decade long discussion/debate/arguments about leveling the playing field. You have always encouraged me to be bold when I wanted to be careful. You have taught me about the power of purpose and passion and about the courage it takes to stick your neck out for your principles on a daily basis. Your voice is in this book as much or more than mine, and I am grateful everyday for you.

Contents

Foreword

DR. SARA GOLDRICK-RAB

Change is never easy. As a sector, higher education has experienced massive changes over the last fifty years. Education beyond high school used to be uncommon, an activity only undertaken by people with significant financial resources and time. Today most high school graduates go on to some sort of additional education or training, and many adults who didn't do that right out of school are now returning.

As a result, most institutions of higher education have an entirely new role. Sifting and winnowing among students to select only those easiest to graduate is rarely acceptable, outside of a few flagrantly wealthy places. All the other colleges and universities will only thrive if they meet students where they are, giving them care and respect, and helping them learn. That requires faculty, staff, and administrators prepared to use every possible tool, often going well beyond the classroom, to provide meaningful support.

Over the last 20 years, as I moved from being a student to becoming a professor and a researcher in this sector, I had the tremendous privilege of getting to know some of incredible humans stepping up to do this work. Chad Dull is among those people, and his new book solidifies his burgeoning role as an inspiring national leader. Embracing uncertainty, willing to grow and change, Dull is showing us all what it really means to do student centered work.

For him, that work began by digging deep into understanding poverty, a topic whose depth went beyond his expectations. I experienced a similar journey when I began to explore affordability in the college setting. What I was told was primarily an issue of rising college tuition turned out to really be about living expenses—it is unaffordable rent, not high tuition, driving so many people deeply into debt and away from college. Learning that helped me find my way to students who gave voice to the unspoken truths: going to college without sufficient funds leads to far worse things than attending class without a textbook. Millions of students cannot afford to eat on a regular basis or enjoy a safe place to sleep.

Many college leaders dismissed these facts when I began amplifying students' stories and sharing the results of my research and teaching on basic needs insecurity. That's why I sought to build a broader movement of people who could collaborate to inform, innovative, and propel social changes needed to support students as humans first. Dull was among the first to join in the #RealCollege movement. This book tells the story of what happened next.

One thing I really appreciate is Dull's honesty about his journey to understanding poverty. Many Americans fall prey to the myth that poverty is the fault of individuals, that it is a characteristic of their cultures, or an artifact of their moral failures. Despite abundant science, even college administrators, faculty, and staff repeat those falsehoods. I'm glad that Dull pushes further to illustrate the many structural constraints, embedded in daily practices and small-policies that create, exacerbate, and/or magnify student poverty. This sort of clarity and transparency will help readers of this book learn and grow as well.

As a boxer I welcome the opportunity to learn new things that refine the way I approach life every day; it helps me adjust my stance and grounds me. It makes it possible to push forward towards another day in the battleground that is higher education with optimism and gratitude. This book is by a learner, for learners. I hope it helps you in your work too.

Dr. Sara Goldrick-Rab is a scholar-activist whose pathbreaking research, teaching, and advocacy has changed how higher education understands and supports college students. A sociologist, she focuses on reducing poverty by revealing unheard truths and sharing that knowledge with multiple publics. Goldrick-Rab's award-winning book, *Paying the Price: College Costs, Financial Aid, and the Betrayal of the American Dream*, documents the failures of policymakers and higher education institutions to make college affordable. Her scientific studies identifying and addressing college students' basic needs for food, housing, childcare, transportation, and health supports sparked the internationally-known #RealCollege movement and inspired federal and state data collection and legislation, as well as countless privately-funded programs.

Goldrick-Rab has founded, led, and supported the growth of multiple organizations transforming higher education. In 2013 she founded the Wisconsin HOPE Lab, and for almost a decade oversaw its growth into The Hope Center for College, Community, and Justice, a 50-person national university center with an annual budget of more than $8M. In 2016 she founded Believe in Students, a national nonprofit that distributed more than $2M in emergency aid to students during the pandemic and empowers faculty to become powerful educators that recognize their students are humans first. In 2019 she translated her research findings into a product that makes it possible for low-income people to access emergency support quickly and with dignity; that work is now advanced by Beam, a Brooklyn-based company.

The recipient of many awards, Goldrick-Rab has appeared on The Daily Show with Trevor Noah and won the $100,000 Grawemeyer prize, which she distributed to students around the country. In 2016, POLITICO magazine named Goldrick-Rab one of the top 50 people shaping American politics. She earned a Carnegie Fellowship, a William T. Grant Foundation Faculty Scholars Award, the American Educational Research Association's Early Career Award, and in 2021 she was named a Monumental Alumna by George Washington University. As a university professor, Goldrick-Rab earned tenure at the University of Wisconsin-Madison and spent nearly 20 years there and at Temple University.

Having retired from academia in 2022, Goldrick-Rab now collaborates, mentors, and writes with people and organizations around the world as CEO of EduOptimists. She also serves as senior fellow at Education Northwest and teaches Sociology 101 at the Community College of Philadelphia. Her next book, *Real College*, is under development.

Preface

BACKGROUND

My life to this point has been informed and defined by poverty. I grew up poor. I didn't always know that, so it took me a long time to recognize and accept. I know now that growing up poor is my defining characteristic. On one level, this doesn't make sense, because it has been 25 years since I had any real financial difficulty. So, in my head, poverty is something in the rear-view mirror and shouldn't really be a factor now. In reality, it will always be a factor in how I see the world, interact with others, and what I value. I could tell you much more about the embedded shame around poverty (and I will later), but for now, know it caused me to believe you don't talk about being poor except in the past tense. Being poor was something you tried to overcome, and if you didn't, well there must be something wrong with you.

But I always knew inside, that couldn't be right...

So, I began a career as a teacher, which former poor kids often do. And I looked around my classroom of seven-year-olds and could all too often see their fate mostly determined by their circumstances. But I didn't really know what to do, so I cared for them, taught as best a new teacher could, and worried about them. I also tried not to think too much about it, because it can eat you up. And I wondered what would happen to them after they left my space each night and at the end of the year. It was always about poverty, but I didn't really name it back then. I moved on to another school, saw the same things, had the same feelings, but still wasn't sure what to do.

POVERTY IS A CIRCUMSTANCE AND A CONTEXT, NOT A CHARACTER FLAW.

It was after I made the transition to working in adult education when I became more vocal about what I was seeing and what I knew. I read books on poverty and made sure in meetings to point out the influence of poverty when it was being ignored or dismissed (which felt like nearly always), but I was just raising awareness and advocating for opportunity. I was doing what I knew how to do, but I knew it wasn't enough. This gained me a reputation as "the poverty guy," but I don't know that I was driving much change. I was in middle management, and so many times we would be discussing a topic, and someone would say something about poverty, and then everyone would look at me and nod, like it had been taken care of. It was frustrating. So, I got someone in Human Resources to send me to a workshop to become an in-house trainer on the issue of poverty. It was great, and I personally trained over 400 people. Awareness was raised, but we seemed stuck at awareness. I wasn't sure we were actually accomplishing much.

As my frustration grew, my need to do something did as well. Attending a high powered meeting where I was asked for my vision of where I wanted to take the college, I talked extensively about becoming a "poverty-informed" college so we could serve students better. Poverty-Informed wasn't a phrase I had heard before, but it aligned verbally with being "trauma-Informed" which was gaining some traction in education circles. Well, I knew I wasn't going to get far, at least at this meeting, when the leader responded, "I am not sure what being 'poverty-informed' is."

My heart sank at his words, but I wasn't upset, frustrated, or even dismayed. Instead, I felt empowered. From that meeting on, I found a new professional vision and purpose. Awareness wasn't enough. If people weren't already aware that poverty was a barrier for students, then I wasn't sure they ever would be. The time for awareness was over, we needed action. But what would that look like? This was often the point where paralysis would strike, and the status quo would just stay in place, but I wouldn't let that happen this time. I resolved to focus on my sphere of influence and try to translate my beliefs into action even if I wasn't sure exactly what to do. I wanted to shift to a bias for doing something.

Shifting to action was the decision. I decided to document progress. This led to a series of essays/articles on LinkedIn. I had no expectations the articles would ever be read by anyone other than a few close friends. Imagine my surprise when those articles were read by tens of thousands of people, led to speaking engagements around the country, and ultimately to this book.

Before you go further into this book, it is important to me to acknowledge this is a work written from the point of view of a white, straight, cis-gender man. I know the identities I carry affect the way I view these issues because I bring the entirety of my life experience. I also want to state unequivocally that racism is real and it is powerful. You cannot divorce issues of race from issues of poverty, and I do not claim my personal experiences allow me to fully understand how differently people of color experience poverty. Rather I commit to continuing to learn. I commit to doing better when I know better. Race and poverty are inextricably linked, and I commit to being an ally and accomplice to people who are marginalized at every opportunity.

PURPOSE

What you are about to read is a practitioner's book, and I own every up, down, and in-between in it. This book will not give you a prescribed program that solves poverty. If that existed, we would have shared that already. Instead, this book:

- Defines Poverty Informed Practice as both a personal practice and method to be used in the classroom.
- Details how Poverty Informed Practice deepens educator's understanding of socio-economic disadvantage and helps sensitize them to school practices that exacerbate inequality.
- Reviews research on how Poverty Informed Practice enhances educators' relationship with students living in poverty of all ages, including those in higher education, and how these strengthened relationships improve student's educational achievement.
- Communicates through real life stories the essential features of Poverty Informed Practice.
- Suggests several practical ways Poverty Informed Practice can be implemented on a school wide basis.

AUDIENCE

Poverty Informed Practice In the Classroom will appeal to a wide range of educators including:

- Teachers and administrators who are unfamiliar with the concept of Poverty Informed Practice.

- Teachers and administrators who serve in high poverty schools and consider themselves well trained and experienced on the topic.
- Educators from high income schools with a small population of low income students.
- School counselors, nurses, specialists, office personnel, school board members, social workers, clergy, parents, coaches. Literally anyone working with a student population.
- Staff and faculty at open access colleges, such as community and technical colleges.

CHAPTER 1

FIRST THINGS FIRST

Psychology and Injustice of Poverty

Deficit Model and Other Popular Myths

I have been writing articles on LinkedIn about Poverty Informed Practice since the summer of 2018. But of course, I've been engaged with this issue of poverty for much longer than that. When I think about it, I am struck by the number of angles I have examined it from. I have my own lived experience of course, but that just reflects my own situation. In addition, I have seen poverty intersecting with education across the spectrum starting as a student, and then in my own career. Here are my thoughts on the psychology of poverty after a lifetime of wrestling with it.

First, we spend a lot of time working from deficit models. This is born directly from the long standing belief in our culture that if you are poor, it is your fault. Blaming the poor for their poverty isn't new, it dates back to at least the English Poor Laws of the 1500s and probably well before that. We treat poverty as a character flaw and all too often this appears in how we try to address the issue. We perform "needs and assets" surveys, but our conversation is all about the needs. Sometimes, we describe our work as "additive" rather than "deficit-minded," but this is just semantics, the solution is to add what is supposedly missing. This kind of thinking keeps our work focused on the individual, rather than the systemic barriers that create and perpetuate poverty. Think about it, if the solution to escaping poverty was just a correct set of behaviors, we would have identified and taught those behaviors long ago. So, I think we need to work from a strengths-based place with individuals, and work on the deficits of the systems which prevent them from moving ahead.

Second, the whole system is rigged. This point was thoughtfully made by Matthew Desmond in his book Poverty by America (Desmond 2023). Poverty by America is a great examination of why money alone alleviates poverty, but not as well as we want. Systems are set up to exploit the poverty of individuals. This includes bank fees, payday lending, exorbitant housing costs paired with a lack of public housing and multiple other systems which conspire against moving people out of crisis and into stability. These systems are so deeply ingrained, we struggle to even see them at times. When you combine invisible systemic barriers with a history of making poverty an individual failing, you get the feelings of hopelessness I observe again and again. People are trapped in a system, but when they complain, they are accused of just not working hard enough. It reminds me of my friend who talked about going to the grocery store with her food stamp card. She said if her cart was filled with treats, she ran the risk of someone accusing her of eating junk on their dime, but if she stocked up with fresh produce and other higher priced foods, she would hear comments about how it must be nice to have the government pay for food others can't afford. It is a great example of the no win situation poverty so often is. For those of us working with people trying to work their way out,we should start with acknowledging this reality.. Beating a rigged system is hard.

Third, my advice to all of us working in this sector is get over yourself. I don't mean that we don't have good intentions, but after 20 years of looking at this issue, it's complicated and takes all of us working together. K-12 can't do it alone. Colleges can't do it alone. Social Services can't do it alone, and very rarely can individuals do it alone. As I grow and learn about collective impact, it is clearer to me every day that our parochial interests and sense of how "special" we are in each of our sectors does not matter to people in the crisis of poverty. It is irrelevant to them, and on occasion, incomprehensible. We need to let our agencies play to their strengths, and we need to make things seamless for those we serve. This may mean letting go of our pet project or of being recognized as THE reason someone else succeeds. The other way we need to get over ourselves refers back to observation number one about doing real asset work. All too often, we define "success" for people in poverty by seeing how much closer they are to acting like us. There is nothing magical about middle class values, they are just the dominant values. We need to get over ourselves, see the strengths in the people we serve, and aid them in building on those strengths in ways that work for them, not necessarily what reflects us.

For example, early on when I was trying to move my campus to be action oriented and move beyond awareness of poverty, I was very focused on food access issues. At the same time I was on fire about food pantries and grab and go food, my hero Sara Goldrick-Rab was writing and tweeting things like, "we aren't going to food pantry our way out of this problem". It made me a little frustrated and defensive at the time, but I totally get it now. In my community impact work, there is a lot of focus on food drives, coat drives, and access to other necessary services. These are all important and required, but they aren't solutions to poverty. They are mitigation. Mitigation matters, but it doesn't do very much to solve root cause issues. We can expand and grow food pantries and someone won't be hungry that day or week, but we aren't dealing with why they are hungry in the first place or providing lasting solutions. So Dr. Goldrick-Rab was right. You can see again, we make poverty an individual problem and that is corrosive. People in poverty are conditioned to believe they did something wrong, and are treated like they did as well. The system feels rigged, because in many ways it is. And because we treat poverty as an individual problem, we use fragmented solutions when we need collaborative collective impact.

Early Poverty and Education Research

Dr. Ruby Payne and Dr. Donna Beagle are well known early researchers defining and understanding the psychology of poverty and its relationship to education. I've been trained and certified by both Dr. Payne and Dr. Beegle's organizations, and I credit them for bringing attention to the poverty crisis, helping me to better understand it, providing me with credentials and a platform to be 'the poverty guy,' and adding fuel to my lifelong interest in the topic.

DR. RUBY PAYNE

Dr. Payne turned the spotlight on how children in poverty think, behave, and have formative experiences that differ from those born into wealth. Much of her work focuses on helping people in poverty understand and use the rules of the middle class to get ahead. (Payne, R. 1996).

DR. DONNA BEEGLE

Dr. Beegle, a child of poverty, uses research and deep lived experience to help create awareness of what it is to live in the crisis of poverty. She helps those without lived experience gain empathy and understanding. Her research has shed light on the proven benefits of raising awareness beyond stereotypes and judgment to provide genuine educational opportunities while training countless educators through Communication Across Barriers poverty and coaching institute (Beegle, D. 2000).

Awareness to Systemic Action

DR. GOLDRICK-RAB

Dr. Goldrick-Rab and her research teams have done considerable work shifting to a system focus while dispelling the myths we know as the mainstream psychology of poverty, which is to treat poverty as an individual problem. Here are a few research highlights:

- A 2016 study of 13 public universities across Wisconsin found that offering students additional grant aid increases the odds of bachelor's degree attainment over four years, helping to diminish income inequality in higher education (Goldrick-Rab, S., Kelchen, R. et. al 2016).
- Originating in 2018, #RealCollege survey is the nation's longest running annual assessment of basic needs insecurity among college students. The 2020 report shows that 39% of respondents were food insecure in the prior 30 days; 46 percent were housing insecure in the previous year; and 17 percent of respondents were homeless in the previous year (Baker-Smith, C, Coca, V, Goldrick-Rab, S. et. al 2020).
- In 2019, Dr. Goldbrick-Rab and a new research team determined that campus food pantries are not enough to address the substantial food insecurity among the college population (20-50% vs 12% general US population). What was more effective was to use the food pantry as a first point of contact to assist eligible students to enroll in SNAP (Supplemental Nutritional Assistance Program, formerly known as food stamps and the nation's largest food benefit and poverty reduction

program). It wasn't pep talks, individualized applications, capability screenings or other hoops to jump. The highly scrutinized and controversial financial aid system and easing access to programs like SNAP are most effective (Freudenberg, N., Goldrick-Rab, S. et. al 2019).

DR. RUSSELL LOWERY-HART

Dr. Russell Lowery-Hart is a renowned academic leader who served as President of Amarillo College in Amarillo Texas 2014-2023 and received the prestigious Aspen Prize for Community College Excellence, which is the nation's signature recognition of high achievement and performance among America's 1,100 plus community colleges.

If you aren't familiar with Amarillo, it's a high poverty city with more than half of its residents (54%) in need of significant financial aid and 70% of Amarillo College students being first generation college students. Dr. Lowery-Hart is renowned because under his leadership: Amarillo College committed to meeting, knowing, and (yes) loving their students to success. Knowing students meant understanding their true needs. Then they built systems around those needs. As a result, three year completion rates rose from 22% to 56% in five years, all from what I call the poverty informed practices of understanding needs then taking action to address them in a timely fashion (Martin, G. and Ardoin, S. 2023).

POVERTY INFORMED PRACTICE - HARD, BUT NOT COMPLICATED

Grounded in current research, Poverty Informed Practice differs from prior programs by taking the hard, but non-complicated approach to be more invested in changing systems to better accommodate the people they serve, rather than asking people to adjust to systems not designed for them. Poverty Informed Practice challenges individuals and organizations to take action and move away from deficit-based models. It treats poverty as a true crisis. Again, this is a way for systems to get ready for the people they serve and not the opposite.

IT'S NOT COMPLICATED,
IT'S HARD.

Invitation to Action

I discovered Neil Young when I was in college. I was about 25 years late to the game, but in the fall of 1989, I heard "Rockin' in the Free World" for the first time. I love music, but like my dad, I'm a lyrics guy at heart, and even in my teen years, there were lyrics in this song that put me in discomfort. In the 2nd verse, Neil describes seeing a "woman in the night with a baby in her hand." The woman "put her kid away" while she struggles with her addiction, and the song says she "hates her life and what she's done to it..." This part always made me uncomfortable and emotional. I didn't have language for it then, but I knew what it was to have someone you love struggle with addiction, and the way they felt about themselves, and how it was reinforced by a world that blames you for your struggles. But it was what Neil sang about the child that has stuck with me for more than 30 years, "There's one more kid that'll never go to school, never get to fall in love, never get to be cool..." For someone just out of high school, this felt so unfair, so viscerally wrong. How can children be robbed of their chance? How could we allow that to happen? I think it is why I chose my first career as a teacher. I wasn't very sophisticated, but I just knew this was not right or fair.

The struggle comes in asking ourselves: Where does my right to have things run into the fact others have so much less? Where do my choices to take care of myself mean I am ignoring the needs of others? And perhaps even more sinister, where do I turn my gaze from systems that benefit me, even if they harm others? For me, this raises big questions. I think it is remarkable that those who are being excluded aren't even angrier than they are. Do we keep restrictions on what we will do to even the playing field because it might put us at risk? What are those of us who believe the status quo is not okay, willing to actually put on the line? There are times I think the kind of change we need can only happen at a policy level, but I wonder if that is an easy excuse for those of us who have what we need to live. I have more questions than answers, but today I am confident a quote from Russell Lowery-Hart in the Atlantic is on the money. "It isn't enough, we're not doing enough, we have to do more." I am committing to doing more, and risking more, will you? (Bombardieri, M. 2018).

CHAPTER 2

INTRODUCING THE FUNDAMENTALS

Poverty Informed Triangle

So, now that we have explored the psychology and injustice of poverty, what are we doing here?

I suppose people could call it many things, but to me; it is building poverty-informed classrooms, schools and colleges based on fundamentals included within the **Poverty Informed Triangle:** meeting basic needs, creating a sense of belonging, and supporting people just when they need it to accelerate their progress.

Why Start With Fundamentals?

My original dream job wasn't academic administration, shocking as that may be. From the time I was ten years old, I had a love affair with the game of basketball. In truth, my 5'8" frame and slow feet made it more of a love/hate affair, but it was always there.

I went to a very small high school, so my lack of physical gifts didn't prevent my participation even though my dad (a very successful high school coach) told me my greatest athletic asset was my... brain. I think he meant it as a compliment. But I loved the game a lot and after heading off to college, I declared an education major in part for the opportunity to give back through athletics. Over the past 30 years, I've coached at the youth level, high school level, and small college level. My coaching record won't put me in anyone's Hall of Fame, but I've learned some very important lessons. I learned relationships are the real reason most of us love athletics, and I learned my own strengths and limitations (I'm a hellacious recruiter, but not a great practice planner for example). But what I learned more than anything is my coaching was always trumped by talent. If players couldn't play, my contribution was really in the margins in terms of winning and losing. And the ability to play always came down to the ability to dribble, pass, shoot, and defend. These are the fundamental skills of basketball, and without them, it's hard to even get started. So, when my teams struggled, we always went back to basics, to fundamentals.

What does this have to do with poverty informed practice? I'm guessing you see the parallels. This idea of dealing with poverty first is rooted in the idea of working from the fundamentals, the basic building blocks. Without certain fundamentals in place, moving people ahead through school is very hard to impossible. The student stories I hear most aren't about difficulty with course materials or complaints about the quality of instruction. I think of a student I know who lived in seven different residences in a year, including time sleeping outdoors. What gets in the way of their success are threats to their fundamental needs as human beings as identified in the three parts of the Poverty Informed Triangle. Listen carefully and perhaps you'll hear my favorite mantra echoing in the triangle's background: *Every Barrier That Can Be Removed, Should Be Removed.*

My younger self learning the fundamentals

1 Meet Basic Student Needs

First, we recognize basic needs impact persistence and graduation, and we work relentlessly to meet those needs or partner with those who can help us do so. We refuse to lose someone because of their resource limitations. Resources, or basic physiological and safety needs including air, water, food, shelter, sleep, clothing, reproduction, personal security, employment, resources, health, property; as famously defined through Abraham Maslow's Hierarchy of Needs (Maslow, A., & Lewis, K. J. 1987) Educators often discuss a framework known as Bloom's taxonomy to organize instruction from basic memorization to more complex synthesis and analysis. In a poverty-informed approach, we acknowledge that Maslow will always precede Bloom.

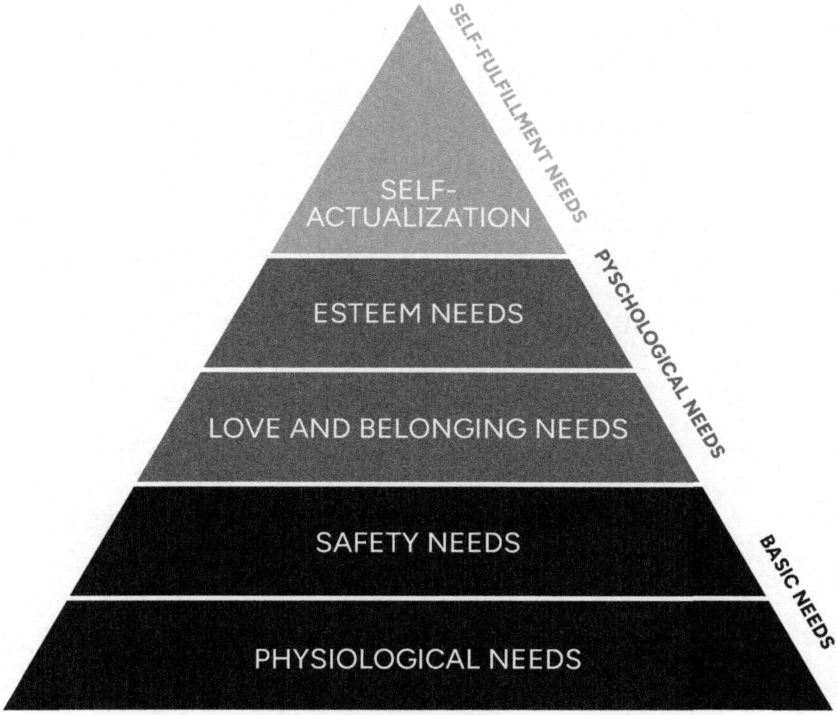

MASLOW'S HIERARCHY OF NEEDS

WHAT THE RESEARCH SAYS

- According to the 2021 US Census Bureau, the official US poverty rate was 11.6% which includes 17% of all children in the United States, a staggering 12.2 million kids total. A family of four with annual earnings below $27,479 is considered poor. In the last decade, the percentage of U.S. children in poverty has risen from 18% in 2008, peaked at 23% in 2011 and 2012, and fell to 17% in 2019.

- New Hampshire has claimed the No. 1 spot in overall child well-being, followed by Massachusetts and Iowa. Mississippi, Louisiana and New Mexico sit at the other end of this list. In fact, save for California and Alaska, the lowest 18 ranked states call Appalachia, the South or the Southwest home (Source: https://www.aecf.org/resources/2019-kids-count-data-book).

- As previously mentioned, the 2020 #RealCollege survey report shows that 39% of respondents were food insecure in the prior 30 days; 46 percent were housing insecure in the previous year; and 17 percent of respondents were homeless in the previous year (Baker-Smith, C, Coca, V, Goldrick-Rab, S. et. al 2020).

- 1 in 10 students from generational poverty–poverty present for at least two generations– complete post secondary training programs due to poverty related obstacles. That dismal statistic is even lower for former foster care children: only 3% (Beegle, D. 2000).

Connection → Basic Needs and School Achievement

- Students who report not having basic needs met are more likely to have diminished academic achievement including lower GPA, behavioral problems, isolation from social networks, mental health concerns and overall poorer self-rated general health (Hagedorn-Hatfield, RL, Hood, LB & Hege, A. 2022).

Why Meeting Basic Needs in the Classroom Is Hard but Not Impossible

Part of what we are doing here is acknowledging students are humans first and working to create the conditions where learning is possible. Learning while you are hungry or unsure where you will sleep is a tall order. Poverty-informed educators make small strides, step-by-step decisions, to be mindful of and support their student's basic needs, steps that do not require abundant resources or time. See part 3 of this book for real life examples.

HOW IT WORKS IN REAL LIFE

Keeping the Lights On

Our community college team made the decision to give access to campus during COVID even after we moved to distance learning. We knew the food pantry was indispensable for many of our students, and we knew technology access was not a given as we moved more online. So, we left a skeleton crew on campus, used every spacing and cleaning protocol we could, and stayed open to students for support if not for classes. I realize this might be controversial, but not everyone is safer at home, and not everyone can delay their dream. We did what we had to, because parking lot WiFi for people without devices was not an acceptable solution.

2 Create Sense of Belonging

The second principle is about creating a sense of belonging in the campus or classroom. This is working on what our facilities "say," how our staff interact, and making sure our students can see people like them represented on campus. This means we must make our staff more representative of the students we are reaching out to. It also means we need to look at our facilities, the artwork, the pictures, and the language and words we use in our signs and on our documents. We want to create a place that screams "you belong here."

In other words, creating environments beyond the transactional and obligatory welcome to spaces where students know they are wanted. It might seem small, but I think it's an important distinction. If you are somewhere in my age range, you can remember when we used the word tolerance a lot talking about diversity and inclusion. When I think about that word now, it seems so patronizing to tell someone you would tolerate their differences from you. My prediction is we will feel the same way about the word "welcome" before too long. Welcome is the lowest bar.

Let's get ahead of the game by moving beyond everyone is welcome to making sure students know they are wanted, especially if they have felt unwanted elsewhere. It goes beyond poverty, but it is definitely informed by poverty. Students in the crisis of poverty often feel as if they aren't really supposed to be on campus; we are going to make sure they know it is exactly where we **want** them to be. And it has me thinking about other well-intentioned efforts many of us get wrong.

WHAT THE RESEARCH SAYS

- The more high-poverty students know and relate to other students, the more likely they are to participate in extracurricular and other activities known to enhance school retention and achievement. Also increased relatedness or sense of belonging to others at school reduces depressive symptoms (Bouchard, M., Denault, A. S., & Guay, F. 2023).
- Social belonging interventions have been shown to improve academic outcomes for high school students (Williams, C. L., Hirschi, Q. 2020).

Connection ⟶ Basic Needs and School Achievement

- Extensive bodies of research by educational think tanks like CASEL (casel.org) and Stanford Graduate School of Education (ed.stanford.edu) stress fostering belonging as it positively relates to school achievement in grades prek-12.
- Creating a sense of belonging in the first days of college has been shown to be crucial for students' academic success, emotional well-being and overall college experience (Castro 2021).

HOW IT WORKS IN REAL LIFE

If you try to remember mentors who made a difference in your life, they probably did lots of things. I've been lucky enough to have several good mentors, but they all had one characteristic in common. For me, they created a sense of safety, which was really another way of saying they made me feel like I belonged where I was. If you accept the Poverty Informed Practice premise that we must love the students we have (not the ones we wish we had), how would you create the same experience for them? Would you be vulnerable enough to let them know a little bit about you in case they see themselves in your story? Would you fearlessly inventory your policies, practices, behaviors, facilities, and anything else you could identify to make sure there aren't messages of exclusion? This is the work it takes to begin to change our current outcomes and benefit our students, their families, and our communities.

Not Just Welcome, Wanted

Anyone who has been in education for any length of time has students who are simply stuck in our head and will be forever.

My career in education started a long time ago as a grade school teacher, and I often think of a boy in my first class of 19 second graders - we'll call him Bradley. Bradley often showed up at school in worn out or dirty clothes, and his family seemed to be going through a lot of tough times. He told me stories of having to sleep in one room of the house because the heat was off, or about the time the sewer back up made part of the house unusable.

Anyone who has been a teacher has had a kid like Bradley in their class. You do what you can to help, but Bradley and his family's troubles aren't the first thing I remember about him. I remember a little boy who simply could not stay quiet. In fact, he said his first-grade teacher told him he was a "blurter," as in he would blurt things out without thinking. That teacher was right. Bradley did blurt things out, all the time, but he was thinking. We had a very familiar pattern. I would be teaching a lesson and often from across the room,

I would hear, "Uhm Mr. Dull ... " And I would sigh and answer, "Yes, Bradley". And without fail, he would respond "I like you, Mr. Dull", and I would smile and reply, "I like you too, Bradley."

So, why am I telling you this? I am sharing this story because it has shaped what I believe students of all ages need. Bradley was a young person in tough circumstances who needed a place to belong. Our little banter about liking one another was him verifying he was wanted in my classroom and in our school. Looking back, I think he was afraid people didn't want him to be there because he wasn't great at following rules, and school was hard for him. Making sure we liked each other (daily) was his way of checking. Poverty Informed Practice means letting our students know daily that of course they are welcome here, but more than that, you are wanted.

POVERTY INFORMED PRACTICE MEANS LETTING OUR STUDENTS KNOW DAILY THAT OF COURSE THEY ARE WELCOME HERE, BUT MORE THAN THAT, YOU ARE WANTED.

A Word About Professional Distance

Over the years as I've developed my own Poverty Informed Practice, I have given up a lot of the professional distance I used to maintain, and I'm encouraging you to do the same. I should be perfectly clear, we must all still be professional and ethical, but I think we have to be willing to let down our walls a little and let the student stories into our world. Being connected to the "why of the what" allows us to persevere when student journeys are non-linear, and on the days where our emotional investment leaves us in a place of vulnerability. Just this week, I had to deal with the fact that a couple of students I had been pretty close to (in my prior life and in my new one) did things which were just not okay. Not only did that hurt me at a personal level, I'm always fearful it will lead to others thinking the work of including these students isn't worth it.

That is the emotional risk of choosing to love the students you have and believing in them unconditionally. Sometimes it doesn't work out. I used to worry a lot more about these things, but in recent years, my answer is "So what?". We don't stop doing the right thing because someone else didn't. We don't assign one person's behavior to an entire group (or we certainly shouldn't). This work can be lonely and uncomfortable on those days, and make no mistake there are people out there waiting for those moments of struggle to push you back to where you were. Can you imagine how the students feel in the same scenario? That's why creating a sense of safety and genuine belonging matters every day. That's why we do things alongside our students, and not just on their behalf.

3 Just in Time Support

Time can be the enemy for the students we serve. This is why talk of "gap years" sits uneasy in my mind. While it sounds sensible hearing an 18 year old say they need to work for a year or so to save money for college, in reality the longer you defer a dream, the higher the odds of life intervening and derailing the dream. In this case, the very high stakes dream of education. Early intervention or support of K12 leads to higher probability of attaining college certificates and degrees that we know provide poor kids with their best chance to raise incomes breaking the poverty cycle. So, we are committed to honoring what people have done and know when they arrive, and moving them quickly to a place of stability, success, and next steps.

TIME IS THE ENEMY FOR PEOPLE IN POVERTY.

WHAT THE RESEARCH SAYS

- A robust body of evidence exists supporting early intervention for impoverished children. Negative outcomes arise through gaps in education. Thus, we have national programs like HEAD START, and it's reasonable to conclude time is of the essence when it comes to education and children of poverty (Yeh, C. T., & Wodtke, G. T. 2023).
- Slowing down or 'holding back' students in school is another failed approach to help poor kids. The results of a 2022 cross National multi-level analysis of students in secondary school retained or kept an additional year in the same grade revealed retained students have a significantly lower sense of belonging, particularly in schools where very few students are retained. That lack of belonging (see #2!) has implications such as behavioral issues and ultimately a higher dropout rate. (Van Canegem, T., Van Houtte, M., & Demanet, J. 2022).

Connection → Basic Needs and School Achievement

- For community college students, the longer the list of non-credit developmental or pre-work requirements to start college, the higher the dropout rate. According to Columbia Research Center in New York, NY, the annual cost of providing remediation to community college students nationwide has been estimated at approximately $7 billion. Only 28 percent of community college students who take a developmental education course go on to earn a degree within eight years, and many students assigned to developmental courses drop out before completing their sequence and enrolling in college-level courses.
- The U.S. Bureau of Labor Statistics (BLS) notes that workers with a postsecondary degree or training certificate typically earn more than those with only a high school education. Exponentially more, according to the data ("Education pays, 2021," Career Outlook, U.S. Bureau of Labor Statistics, May 2022).

HOW IT WORKS IN REAL LIFE - PART ONE

Poverty Informed practice requires progress and supporting people "just-in-time." Much of the support is academic, but for me it broadens out to emergency support and basic needs support as well. I'm pleased to say there are schools all over my state and the country with food pantries, grab-and-go food, and emergency funds to bridge the moments that prevent students from succeeding. But I also know we live in a culture which wants to make poverty a character flaw instead of a context. And because this point of view is baked in deep, we inadvertently build systems in opposition to their stated purpose. Emergency funds are a great illustration of how we can get this wrong in my opinion.

Twenty years ago, I bought into the idea of teaching financial literacy as a primary strategy to help students in a financial crisis. I reject that idea now. I often see emergency funds coming out of offices with the term financial literacy attached to them. Let me be exceedingly clear, financial literacy works very well for people with money, but in my opinion, it is a bankrupt concept (no pun intended) for people in the crisis of poverty. You cannot manage or be literate about that which you do not have and implying that becoming more literate is the solution transfers the blame to the person in crisis. You can see the hard wiring of blaming the poor for being poor. So, when I see emergency funds coupled with financial counseling or with literacy workshops, I get kind of irate. This sort of help feels like lecturing a gunshot victim on ducking faster before you stop the bleeding. It's ineffective at best and damaging at worst. I know a number of students who stopped going for help because it felt dehumanizing. The irony is the people giving out the assistance genuinely see themselves as good people and helpers. I'm angry at myself for my attitude 20 years ago, and I'm angry at so many emergency aid programs today.

So, What Do You Do?

Number One, stop making people ask multiple times for help. Try this instead: if you have the courage and vulnerability to ask, we believe you and get you what you need. If this makes you immediately think people will take advantage, I'd challenge you to examine your view of people. Do you really think people will abuse such a system, and if so, how many? Even if there is a percentage, is it worth building barriers that tell the 95% of people who just need help, we think you are suspect and need to be screened. Do we really think there is a benefit to making them tell their story multiple times, and then wait to see if they qualify? It is an **emergency!** That's why we call them emergency funds.

Number two, critically examine how we talk about the students we serve and the criteria to access these services. Do you know how often I've heard someone referred to as a good bet or bad bet? Isn't that dehumanizing and awful?

Can you imagine having the vulnerability to say you need help, and how you would feel if you knew people went into another room and decided if you were worthy of betting on.

Finally, accept that this is hard. As with so much poverty-informed work, it isn't particularly complicated, it is just hard. Our choice about supporting people just-in-time is as much about changing our mindsets, as it is about figuring out how to deliver the help. Instead of helping as many people as we can with the resources we have, we use a scarcity model to hoard resources and develop systems to decide who deserves help and who doesn't. That is corrosive and toxic in my opinion.

HOW IT WORKS IN REAL LIFE - PART TWO

I worked at a college where we removed all criteria from an emergency fund for GED testing. We simply said if a staff member heard you needed help, you got it. The usage of the fund went up 500%. It strained the resources, but so what? We pursued more resources because we discovered our "criteria" were keeping people from asking. If you have similar systems, you need to ask yourself the big questions. Are you trying to help, or are you trying to pick winners and losers? Do you believe needing help is a normal part of life, or do you see it as a sign of weakness and a character flaw? My point of view is obvious on this one, and even if you aren't entirely sold, think about all the energy and effort wasted to sort out who gets help and who doesn't. What if we just trusted the people we serve and redirected the time we gain to making things better. That is how we treat an emergency.

3

CHAPTER

POVERTY INFORMED PRACTICE

3 Actions to Get Started

CREATING BELONGING
ACCELERATION / JUST-IN-TIME SUPPORT
Poverty
Informed
Triangle
MEETING BASIC NEEDS

1 Declaring the Movement

Michael Sorrell, the President at Paul Quinn College in Dallas, wrote an article in 2018 about making your school a movement. He said his entire college had one goal that defines everything about them: to end poverty. How powerful is that? How brave is it just to say it? It makes you feel guilty for nibbling around the edges. Well our days of nibbling are over, at least in the corner of the world I lead. But how do you begin? In my mind, step one is to say it out loud: declare the movement and your mission, whether that be with our team or on your own.

When I suggest "declaring the movement" by saying it out loud. I mean OUT LOUD. Dr. Beegle uses the phrase "living in the crisis of poverty" (Beegle, D.M. 2003), and crisis is exactly what we are responding to. When we accept the truth of students being in crisis, it makes us more assertive and willing to put ourselves out there for them. I suspect many of you were like me and advocated in gentle, compromising ways to try to win people over. I'm asking you to rethink that. I'm asking you to make the affirmative case that we don't throw people away. I'm asking you to explore being slightly less comfortable, perhaps less widely popular, but far more effective. If I've learned anything, it's a watered down version of purpose gets watered down results, and we don't have time for that.

At my school, we landed on the following mission to address our goal of ending poverty:

"EVERY BARRIER THAT **CAN BE** REMOVED **SHOULD BE** REMOVED."

Our staff immediately grabbed onto the idea. Discussions followed in which we started using shared language and imagery including the analogy of plowing the road (we are from Wisconsin after all). Many of us had people who plowed the road to make our trip safer. Maybe it was well-resourced parents if we were fortunate, or someone else who took an active interest in our success. Perhaps you are a parent who thinks about plowing the road and removing barriers for your own children. All too often, the people we serve traverse roads that aren't plowed or are partially blocked because of the random circumstance they were born into. How is that fair? How much potential is left in tent cities and hungry bellies when we can do something? Every barrier that can be removed, should be removed... Would we do any less for our own children, would our parents have done any less for us? We have an opportunity to level the playing field, and I think we have an obligation to do so.

It certainly didn't happen overnight. In taking step one, declaring a movement, we had a mission for our ending poverty goal. And we have action steps we describe as "plowing the road."

DECLARE A MOVEMENT IN THE CLASSROOM ⟶ PLOW THE ROAD

1. Adding a basic needs statement to course syllabi.
2. Emergency Funds. Changing policy to include as few barriers as possible.
3. Conduct a "No Audit" on signage. A no audit assumes everything speaks. Our facilities, signage, behavior, and everything else on campus is constantly telling students whether they belong. Unfortunately, too many of our students have been getting messages for much of their life that they don't belong and are less than. We began the audit by looking for places we were inadvertently delivering the wrong message. The truth was a bit disheartening. We found signs in all capital letters saying STAFF ENTRANCE ONLY, even though the door was already locked. We found test booklets labeled 'please do not write in the booklet," not real friendly and frankly a little confusing. Before we had even begun to examine our behavior, we found our materials were telling our students to stay out and implied they didn't know how to use an answer sheet. Once you begin to see these unintended messages, you really can't unsee them, and you notice them everywhere. At the last college I worked at we offered poverty-informed training shortly after I was hired. The day we finished, my assistant took the idea of unintended exclusion and found immediate action. His desk and my office were near a door marked "staff entrance only." That day he propped the door open and told me we don't prevent students having access to us or the things they need. It was a powerful moment.

Poverty
Informed
Triangle
CREATING BELONGING
ACCELERATION / JUST-IN-TIME SUPPORT
MEETING BASIC NEEDS

2 Give Voice to Lived Experience

All too often in education, I hear stories that make me think of a kind of tortured Harry Potter analogy. I hear too many conversations where we seem to be functioning as sorting hats rather than advocates for success. If you haven't read Harry Potter, the Sorting Hat is placed on students' heads and assigns them to their house at Hogwarts School. The houses all seem to have a prototypical profile and type and the house they are sorted into has a lot to do with their character arc.

Our education version of sorting students into houses comes out in insidious phrases like "they wouldn't make it at the university" or in behavior that tells students they don't belong because they don't use words the right way or some other hidden rule. Did students have input in how their class runs or was it all preordained? Students in poverty might not meet our norms on day one, but that does not indicate what they are capable of learning. It is all too easy to slide into a place of judgment and decide what people are capable of without ever adding their voice to the conversation.

Our journey to being poverty-informed in our offices and classrooms is going to require us to give greater voice to those we serve as opposed to making sorting hat judgments and leaving potential untapped.

GIVE VOICE TO LIVED EXPERIENCE ⟶ ASK THE MAGIC QUESTION

Dismantling the power differential starts to change the conversation from "this student doesn't have what it takes to succeed" to asking students the all important magic question:

WHAT DO YOU NEED TO SUCCEED?

For example, we were pleased to include a student on a big college trip, and none of us anticipated her panic when we sent her an expense report to get reimbursed for the trip. How do you reimburse someone who has nothing? How many other assumptions did we make? For instance, we assumed this person would meet her group at the airport, until someone offered a ride. So, it was a double edged sword for us.

Clearly, we made mistakes. From those mistakes, we've learned that including the student's voice in our work made us better. That is the fundamental premise of poverty-informed practice. Our students with barriers show us ways to get better more clearly and quickly than other students ever could. So, we must find a way for their voices to be a legitimate part of the conversation.

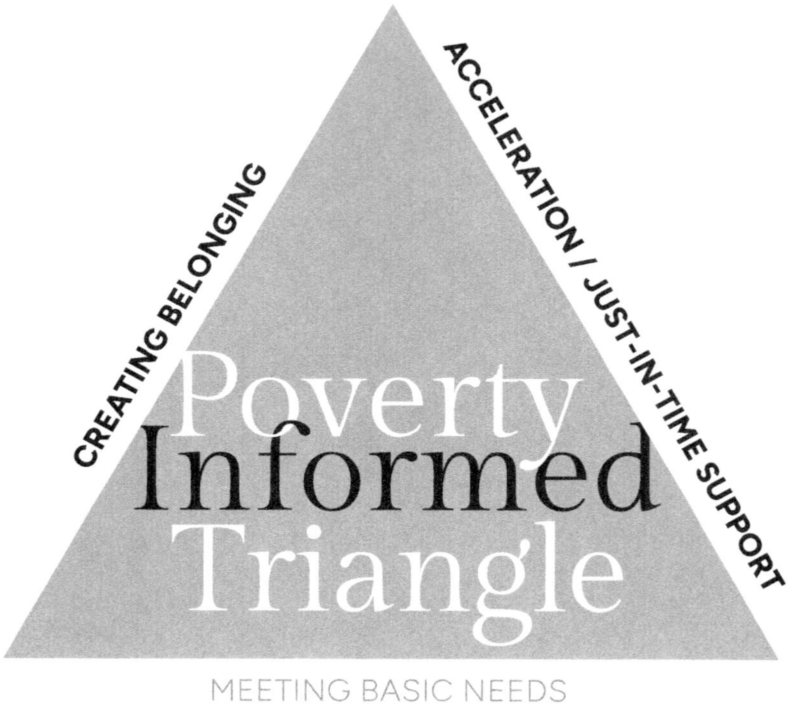
CREATING BELONGING
ACCELERATION / JUST-IN-TIME SUPPORT
Poverty Informed Triangle
MEETING BASIC NEEDS

3 Always Leave a Path Back

I believe everyone deserves another chance. This may be the most controversial statement of the book you are reading. After all, who hasn't worked with that extremely difficult student who you just wanted to give up on, make a plan to send to another school, or kick you out altogether? Education is the best bet for children of poverty to rise up the economic ladder breaking its vicious cycle. Excluding people from it is not a way to help them move forward. Poverty Informed Practice is about believing people deserve another chance, not just a second chance. If we don't believe in students, sometimes before they believe in themselves, the world might miss out on the gifts someone had to give back. Poverty Informed practice does not throw people away, we need everyone.

ALWAYS LEAVE A PATH BACK ⟶ STORY ABOUT MY DAD

My dad, a local legend, has been my greatest teacher about redemption, second chances, and belief. These are lessons I started learning in early elementary school.

My parents had a pretty amicable divorce, and I was able to spend a lot of time with both of them, although the custom of the time meant my mom had primary custody, and I saw Dad on weekends and more in the summer. I remember once Mom dropped me off at an apple orchard where Dad might have been working at the time. He was staying in a tent and had a cook stove, and we had a nice camping adventure. If I'd been a little older, camping in an orchard might have seemed unusual, but it was just an adventure at the time.

Forty years later, I sat at a Dr. Beegle workshop listening to her talk about how her family often "camped" which was just a euphemism for a period of homelessness. At that moment, the light bulb went on. After the workshop, I asked my dad about that visit and sure enough, dad was homeless that summer. In fact, he confessed to me he had actually stolen the tent, and I'm assuming the stove too. I could add this story to my collection of childhood stories demonstrating how situational ethics are and how easy it is to do the so-called right thing when times are good. Dad stole a tree (for those who never stole a tree, it means sneaking on someone's land, cutting it down, and splitting it into firewood before getting caught) once to make sure we had wood to heat the house, and I have a vague recollection of him shooting a partridge once out of season, so we could eat.

Those times were objectively hard I suppose, but I didn't really know that until I was older. Dad was fun and our collection of Volkswagen vans that seemed to not have heaters or occasionally catch fire didn't seem to faze him. He must have been stressed out beyond comprehension, but I don't remember seeing it. In hindsight, I can see the insidious hand of poverty pushing him away from dreams and into choices that made less sense all the time. This came to a head when I was about eight. Poverty causes desperation and as my Dad's family grew, so did his desperation.

My weekend visits to his small home in the middle of nowhere now involved sleeping in the living room because upstairs, the solution to our problems was drying and getting ready for sale. It was the 1970's, so marijuana wasn't an unusual thing in either of my homes, but dad figured out could grow it and could sell it for real money. I remember talk of $10,000 and a trip to Hawaii, but more clearly then that, I remember the day Dad and some friends were sitting at the table playing cards when an army of police arrived in our front yard. Standing outside while they searched the house, they found everything. I froze in fright overhearing the police say I may need to go to foster care until they could reach my mom. Fortunately, mom picked me up and that didn't happen.

Dad was sentenced to thirty days in jail, and I suppose his story should have ended there...but it didn't. After his brief time away, dad decided his real dream was to be a teacher and a coach. An odd choice for a convicted felon, but he believed and belief matters. Dad returning to school suddenly became a family project. I remember a change jar to save for tuition, a Ford Pinto with over inflated tires to get better mileage, a family on a mission, and bringing home Shakespeare books and being on fire as he got a chance to stretch his intellect we all knew he had. Dad is charismatic, and we were all on fire with him. Belief is contagious and people around dad began to believe in him too. Every time money was running out, some would mysteriously show up. Dad later learned his professor took care of parts because of his belief in my dad. That professor changed my life without ever meeting me, and it has inspired me to pay it forward, including the development of an emergency fund honoring the practice of faculty helping students directly.

All of that belief resulted in my dad's thirty year teaching career highlighted by a classroom doorway full of students from the moment he arrived because he created a safe and welcoming space for the most vulnerable kids in the building. He won national recognition for organizing a Renaissance Faire run completely by students. I remember it being written up in USA Today. He is also a basketball coach with nearly four hundred wins, a genuine local legend.

CHAPTER 4

POVERTY INFORMED PRACTICE

4 Actions to Build Momentum

CREATING BELONGING
ACCELERATION / JUST-IN-TIME SUPPORT
Poverty
Informed
Triangle
MEETING BASIC NEEDS

4 Acknowledge the Truth

Use basic needs statements openly and frequently. Basic needs statements are any version of stating to students "if you are having trouble ... because of ... please let me know." For example, "if you are having trouble getting to class because of transportation problems please let me know." This practice not only encourages students to disclose barriers and seek help, it sends a message to them they are not alone. If someone like a teacher says basic needs deficiencies get in the way of school, it must be a common thing and not just me. We must listen to students and accept their reality. For example, low income students often rely on unreliable city buses or parents to get to school. Considering that, it's absurd to have no tolerance policies for being late.

ACKNOWLEDGE THE TRUTH ⟶ SEE THE STUDENTS WE SERVE

Remember the movie Avatar? One of the big emotional payoffs is when the main characters say, "I see you" to one another. It's a substitute for I love you, but it's also more. "I see you," is a South African Zulu greeting made popular in the film. It says, in essence, I see all of you, your light and your darkness, and I am always here for you with respect and love. The response, ngikhona, means I am here. In the Zulu village context, where everyone knows one another, it's a potent representation of understanding, recognition, and compassion.

One of the healing benefits of having these real-world social networks is **that** people really know you—not just your Facebook profile or your bio sketch, but also your dark side, your demons and mistakes, where you messed up. You know they know, and they know you know they know—and they're still there for you. This resonates with me as an advocate for people in the crisis of poverty because I've often found those people to be more interconnected and interdependent than the middle-class norms we have been taught are the ones to aspire to. We have to see one another.

I SEE YOU

I'm not the most academically motivated person you will meet. I understand things like accreditation, curriculum design, program learning outcomes, and the like, but it's never been what feeds my soul in this work. What feeds my soul is the idea that education can help end poverty. And I believe proximity to students and their stories and their humanity is the reminder we need when things get hard.

So what should we do in tough times like natural disasters or other crises to hear our students?

Our COVID era solution at the community college level was pretty basic: we asked. My colleague in Student Affairs at the time shared an affection for our students and a soft spot for those left out. We were both concerned about how students were handling the incredible amount of change thrust upon them, so we sent a one statement survey. It said: "We know this is a challenging time to be a college student. Please let us know both what is working for you and what you are struggling with." It was accompanied by an offer to have one of us contact them if they wanted to talk more. The answers we received were illuminating, and a number of students asked for follow up contact as well as expressing gratitude for the opportunity to be heard and seen.

I wish I could tell you we solved every one of these concerns for students, and everything was on track. It's simply not true. I can say asking and trying to understand the real journey of our students is the correct way to start any intervention. As a higher education professional, these are not comfortable moments, but they are important. If we can't hear and see what is really happening, how do we change the world for these people who trust us to help them chase their dreams?

If we don't acknowledge the truth by seeing the students we serve, really seeing them, it will be too easy to give in to our own fatigue and just do the best we can. But if I could talk to them right now, I would want them to know, I see you... I am because we are. Because I know these things, I know that as much as we are doing, it isn't enough, and we have to do more. Once you really see something, it can't be unseen. What will you do to say "I see you" to students?

CREATING BELONGING
ACCELERATION / JUST-IN-TIME SUPPORT
Poverty
Informed
Triangle
MEETING BASIC NEEDS

5 Have a Bias for Action

Poverty informed Practice is 100% about moving past awareness to action. We want people to identify an issue and address it, not form a committee to consider addressing it. We work in an industry that is uncomfortable with a bias toward action. Our structures are designed to be deliberative and slow. Perhaps this was appropriate at one time, but it simply is not anymore. In a world where education is pretty much a necessity, we don't get to make people wait to get what they need. Instead, we accept the reality that classrooms are places to move beyond acceptance and understanding to actually addressing basic needs getting in the way of learning.

GET COMFORTABLE BEING UNCOMFORTABLE

Taking action on behalf of the people in the crisis of poverty as a Poverty Informed practitioner can be a lonely business. We live in a country where we tend to blame poverty on the poor, and they in turn blame themselves. So, when you try to help people think about it differently, you can be seen as challenging assumptions that are held quite deeply. That can be uncomfortable, but embracing some discomfort seems reasonable in the face of poverty is an urgent and treatable issue.

Complacency is the enemy, and this is why action is important if you are really trying to make a difference. I remember talking to a fellow teacher when I was new in K-12 twenty years ago, and she told me she was working with the "most unmotivated students she'd had in 30 years"... they were first graders, six years old. I immediately called her on it and told her six quick ways I could think of to engage children in their learning. She didn't talk to me the rest of the year. I'm embarrassed to say I toned it down after that and tried to fit in better. In hindsight, I was dead right, and I think she was just dead wrong. I'm guessing most readers think so too and can't believe someone would talk that way about children. But I didn't always live up to that conviction, because it was more comfortable to go along.

**DEVELOP A BIAS FOR ACTION.
IF YOU SEE SOMETHING,
DO SOMETHING.**

HAVE A BIAS FOR ACTION ⟶ AVOID COMPLACENCY

So, I'm getting comfortable with being uncomfortable. You don't have to change jobs, but you better avoid getting complacent. How could you be comfortable when you hear students called dehumanizing things like "Last Minute Larry's" when they come to register shortly before the term starts. How different would the world be if that student had a name and a story? How different would our colleges be if we admired the courage it took to come to us at the last moment and ask us to help change your life? As Poverty Informed Practitioners, making a difference is within our power. So first get comfortable being uncomfortable. Then, take action.

HAVE A BIAS FOR ACTION → MOVE PAST THEORY

Earlier in my career, one of my vice presidents was a nurse by training, and she had a particular way of expressing frustration in meetings. Our main interaction was in deans' meetings which were typically a place of much discussion and debate, but relatively little action. When our VP could no longer take the swirl and inaction, she would announce, "Well, the patient is dead..." meaning that if we were this indecisive in health care, the point of the discussion would have expired. She was 25 years older than me at that time in my career, and I found this mostly funny, but as I get a little more veteran myself, I understand her more every day. There is so much to be done, and so often we choose inaction disguised as planning and deliberation. Make no mistake, it is a choice, and a choice with serious consequences.

The same idea resonates with me as we seem to grant ourselves endless opportunities to learn when in reality we need to act. I remember the time a black student held a campus event showing a movie called Color of Fear and interspersed it with guided discussion and reflection. It was a transformative moment for me in my own work with equity and inclusion, but not in just the obvious ways. It was one of the first times I truly considered my identities as white, as male, as cisgender, and all my other identities. I was having what felt like a revelation about my place in the world not being fully earned by my talents.

As we went into the group discussion, I started sharing my insights about myself and my learning. It was truly a powerful moment for me, but I could feel the irritation from another person in the room, a black man, who was older than me. Letting out a big sigh, he said, "I am glad you are learning, but I am too old to keep waiting for all of you." I felt defensive and embarrassed, but I have never forgotten. He was tired of my need to celebrate my own learning and was reminding me the time to act on social injustices and inequities is now. He was right, and I have tried to be more action oriented since, with mixed results.

A Tale of Two Students

At my child Cameron's 4th grade teacher conference, the teacher told me, "Cameron is a genius you know." It was a very nice thing to say, but to be frank there wasn't much historical evidence of that. Cam has never liked school very much and has pretty much no interest in homework. When I pointed it out, the 4th grade teacher said, "Oh not the kind of genius who does school stuff, but trust me he's a genius." Midwestern modesty says the jury is out on the level of genius, but years later I can confidently say Cam retained a gift for language, is a good person, and still hates playing the school game.

As a high school student, Cam was placed in an honors humanities course, which is a combination of history and English. I'd worked hard to let go of concern about grades and instead focus on learning, but humanities had been the one course where the grades weren't good. Cam was neglecting to complete a number of assignments, and this in turn has led to some tough conversations with his teachers, and the possibility of being moved to a different track. Now, what does this have to do with Poverty Informed Practice and seeing the students we serve? Let me tell you.

At some point, Cameron's teachers reached out to share concerns about his performance. The teacher who wrote was obviously upset, and to be honest the note wasn't very kind. I was told Cam could choose to earn poor grades (as she put it), but distracting behavior would not be tolerated. It was upsetting, but I'm an educator too, so I took a deep breath and sent an email. The email asked for further examples of her concerns. It also pushed back on some of the comments I thought were unfair and ended with an offer to talk by phone or in person. I got an immediate response and followed up with a relatively pleasant phone call. I was empathetic, but made it clear Cam valued the class, and I was more worried about his learning than his GPA. When the teacher expressed concern because Cameron is a college-bound student, I shared that I worked at a college, and he could certainly go there, which I hoped he would. It all ended well, and Cam went on to successfully finish the course.

If I'm honest, this is the type of conversation I've had annually with at least one teacher since my kids started school. I don't make apologies for advocating, but I've always had guilt around it because I am so keenly aware of people who don't have advocates like me. I know having college-educated parents who feel like they are able to talk with school staff gets him the benefit of the doubt, and no one thinks it's unusual. It's just part of the built-in help middle class kids get, and no one thinks twice about it. The longer I work at this notion of being poverty informed, the more insidious it all seems. I'm afraid our systems (like schools) were built on unfair and inequitable principles to begin with, so they are designed to perpetuate those inequities. And that is only mitigated if you have someone who can work the system, like I and other middle-class parents do for our children.

Dr. Beegle often refers to taking action by using your title on behalf of others to navigate the system. I didn't disagree, but it always seemed like a small part of what we could do, but now I feel differently. I think it's actually huge, and if your organization is committing to serving people in poverty better, this is a great low-cost place to begin. There is a gulf of difference between giving people the phone number for a service that can help them and making the call with them. You don't have to have a big title to make this strategy work. I've seen faculty get individuals into homeless shelters after the initial request was denied. I've seen financial aid staff get parents to share FAFSA information when a student couldn't convince them to. It bothers me how well this works, but it is reality. As I said earlier, the system is built on some faulty foundations, so sometimes we need to subvert the system to make it work for the people we advocate for. We've been taught this is cheating when in fact, it's just another version of what I would do for Cameron, and no one ever questions that.

All of this makes me think of another student I'll name Devon. Devon is an adult who has none of the advantages Cameron has, and I think that makes their behavior suspect in situations no one would blink at for my child. Devon reached out to me after being removed from one of her courses due to a confrontation with an instructor. This student comes from generational poverty and her vocabulary and behavior do not indicate her intellectual ability (meaning she doesn't do middle class things). Devon also has a strongly developed sense of what she thinks is fair and what she thinks isn't fair.

On this particular day, Devon believed her instructor was being unfair and would not back down on the topic. The instructor was pulled into an emotional reaction, and unfortunately the exchange ended with the instructor telling the student to "get the f*** out of my class." I'm pretty connected to this student and started getting messages that night about what had happened. Devon decided to drop out of school and had been ordered to stay off campus until the following Monday. I'm not the hero of the story, but I am someone with perceived power who could make phone calls and emails on their behalf to see what could be done. Devon could feel assured people would respond to my inquiries and the issue would be resolved. I spent 20 minutes on the phone and writing emails to key folks, and in the end, she returned to campus to try to finish the term. My title and status simply helped Devon navigate a situation like it would have for Cameron.

My heroes at Amarillo College tell us we have to love our students more than we love our policies. I think this is exactly what they are talking about. When middle class people who understand middle class norms violate policy, they (or their advocates) know how to negotiate and mitigate the response to those policy issues. But all too often for our students from poverty, it is just a confirmation of their powerlessness and a reminder they weren't supposed to be here in the first place, and therefore the end of the road.

Poverty Informed Practice challenges us to have a bias for action. For those of us who are parents, it would simply be the equivalent of what we would do for our children. I like to say that poverty-informed practice is an intentional choice to love the students we have. We do things differently for people we love, including using any tools in our toolbox to navigate a system which does not serve them. If we embrace this, it would remove the guilt of intervening on behalf of students who have nothing. People know what is preventing them from getting where they want to go. Ask them what the barriers are and commit to removing them as fast as possible. Move fast enough and decisively enough so no one ever has to tell you the patient has died waiting for you to act.

Poverty Informed Triangle
CREATING BELONGING
ACCELERATION / JUST-IN-TIME SUPPORT
MEETING BASIC NEEDS

6 Practice Radical Hospitality

People in the crisis of poverty have some remarkable qualities, one of which is a generosity and a sharing culture I remember from my childhood and admire to this day,a generosity stemming from the idea that surviving poverty requires an interdependence. When times are good you help others, because when times aren't good, they will help you.

Building on this culture of generosity, my Poverty Informed Practice trainees are taught early on to take action, action that looks different depending on their work or volunteer setting. For example:

- In higher education, radical hospitality can be shown by placing a grab-and-go food basket in a lobby or other common space for everyone. We do so without judgment and without question. We do it because that is what people do. Food seems to always create community. In this case, it's just snack food, but it represents a culture of caring. It duly serves to meet an immediate need for hunger–hard to learn when you are hungry--and starts to teach us how to be radically hospitable.
- For preK-12, radical hospitality can be shown by putting up images in the classroom that look like our students, to let them know they belong. It can also be stacking services within the school to ease the time consuming process of connecting parents to agency services. Community schools are a popular model growing in our country that embrace many poverty-informed principles. Meeting people where they are (literally in this case) is an acknowledgment that being poor can take up all your time.

PRACTICE RADICAL HOSPITALITY ⟶ GRAB AND GO BOWL

Food for Thought

What does someone have to do to be worthy of your help?

Dr. Beegle suggests asking yourself this question will uncover your bias. Turns out, starting a grab-and-go food bowl at school will do the same thing. When I first introduced the bowl into our higher education department, there was initially dismay as I explained the bowl filled with snacks (not necessarily nutritious but what people enjoy eating) is for anyone and everyone without restrictions. Our food is simply for guests, and we would never limit guests or judge them. I then gave explicit direction:

1. Our requirement to stand in awe of our students also causes us to make sure the food is presented nicely. That means when people bring us leftovers from meetings (interesting how often we feed ourselves as administrators in higher ed), we make sure it isn't just flung on the table but laid out nicely for the guests.

2. Do not correct or chastise students for taking too much or too often. This is an exercise in letting go of judgment and letting go of how we think people should behave.

3. We don't know who they are taking it for, and we don't care. We do not worry about who deserves food, lots of

people deserve food, and this isn't charity.

4. If staff are hungry, then they can help themselves.
5. We don't tell them who provided the food, and we don't ask for gratitude. It's a Poverty Informed Practice not to require others to be grateful to be worthy of our help. It's radical hospitality and community for all.

Pushback followed dismay, in subtle and not so subtle ways. One of the less subtle ways is when people note something we are providing is name-brand rather than generic, or is something they don't buy at their own home. The subtext always feels like we are doing something people don't deserve or is too much, which seems suspect to me. These comments are often couched in the guise of concern about our ability to sustain what we are doing, but to be honest it just doesn't feel right. One lesson of the bowl is that bias runs deep, and I think examining how we react to the bowl is a good way to find our own implicit bias.

In fact, I use it as a way to expose just that conversation. What a great way to ask people in a relatively safe space, about why they feel the way they do. Cool things have happened since introducing the bowl. Other people started bringing things in, which was nice, but not surprising (teachers are good people). We also had cash donations from staff and when we started to share our story on social media, we had donations from the outside. The health promotions director from a regional health system offered to partner up and since then sustainable funds have come in from other internal resources allowing the program to expand to multiple bowls around campus. Another surprising outcome was that the bowl program proved to be utilized by impoverished students 40% more than the campus food pantry. I believe this is because the stigma was removed by opening up the bowl to everyone.

Our commitment to the bowl as hospitality (not charity)

levels the playing field just a little bit and allows us to engage students as the adults they are. I also think for someone like me who grew up with occasional food insecurity, food and love are intertwined. My mom took great pride in feeding us, and even taking us out to eat once a month or so. At her funeral, I told the story of how we went out to eat and how she told us it was to learn how to behave in restaurants. But as an adult, I suspect it was more about showing us we could have what other people did and our struggling circumstances didn't mean we couldn't do things that made us happy. I can feel the connection between food and love to this day. So, if we actually love the students we have, food is one way to show it, creating a subtle but important shift in perception as we begin to view our students as our guests. Wanted, loved, and cared for in every way which connects us in their pursuit of a different future.

Poverty Informed Practice leverages relationships and addresses basic needs at every opportunity. Having snacks in the lobby changes behavior, language, and conversations. It is a small thing with powerful ripple effects.

PRACTICE RADICAL HOSPITALITY ⟶ AGENCY PARTNERSHIPS

Reduce Agency Time

"Don't be happy for me that I overcome these barriers, be mad as hell that they exist in the first place."
- Hazim Hardeman, a child of poverty who became a Rhodes Scholar.

Creating fairness between poor students and others takes on all kinds of forms. The good news is these forms are definable. This is hard work, but not complicated.

Ways to Create Fairness:

- Knowing and creating resources that meet basic needs.
- Honor student strengths and create a sense of belonging at every single opportunity, with intention.
- Provide classrooms that meet students where they are and contain flexibility because their lives and circumstances require it.
- Don't require heroism and endless gratitude to get the things other people received because of a twist of fate.

No one is more tuned into what is fair and what is not than an elementary aged child. Children get angry when things are unfair. Although I am no longer a child, it feels like anger might be the right emotion for now. Anger at unfairness is a great way to keep these issues at the forefront and not retreat to places of emotional safety. So let's love the students we have, but let's stay a little angry too, so we don't forget.

Dr. Payne used research collected over many years through aha! Process (ahaprocess.com) to create a framework for understanding poverty that included "The Mental Model of Poverty". The Mental Model meaning what occupies the thoughts and time of someone in poverty compared to that of those in middle and upper classes (Payne, Ruby K. 2005).

Studying this model, what has stood out to me is the concept of agency time. Agency time occurs after poor people are told "we've got a program for that," and we proceed to require them to spend agency time making appointments, navigating to those appointments then filling out intake forms to prove their poverty. In other words, show their shame. Within The Mental Model of Poverty, agency time is a concept just for poor people. It's not something experienced by middle or upper classes.

So many policies and procedures at our schools and elsewhere are designed around a fear of running out of whatever resource we are distributing. It makes me think of emergency funds that don't get distributed because of a fear of not having enough, or of not giving it to the right people. I often describe what we are trying to do as providing the things my middle-class kids get by default to people who didn't get them by the same accident of birth. Do you know the excess of resources my kids get? Isn't it remarkable we feel like we have to ration things to people who have been left with so much less through no fault of their own? I love my children, but they certainly don't deserve the things people born to tougher circumstances don't. In that frame of mind, it becomes easier to consider ways to lessen agency time or make the agency time that is required for our poor families less burdensome.

ACTIONS TO REDUCE AGENCY TIME

1. School Based Food Pantries. Use the food pantry as a first point of contact to assist eligible students to enroll in SNAP (Supplemental Nutrition Assistance Program, formerly known as food stamps).

2. Eliminate applications or other barriers to receive emergency funds for donated school supplies, books, or other basic needs.

3. Stack school open houses or other community events by partnering with social service agencies to more efficiently link families to resources in a one stop shopping model.

4. Encourage high school student enrollment in Credit for Prior Learning and other college credit bearing programs. These programs are vital to smoothing the transition from high school to higher education for generational poverty students.

5. Become a Community School. Community Schools, according to their website, take a whole child approach to supporting students' educational and whole life success. A major part of this research-backed initiative is to provide integrated student support to reduce agency time and better meet needs by having a mix of offerings facilitated through the school. Examples of offerings include dental care, medical care, mental health care, academic support, and housing assistance. Learn more on the National Education Association's website and community schools.futureforlearning.org (Maier, A. Daniel, J., et al 2017).

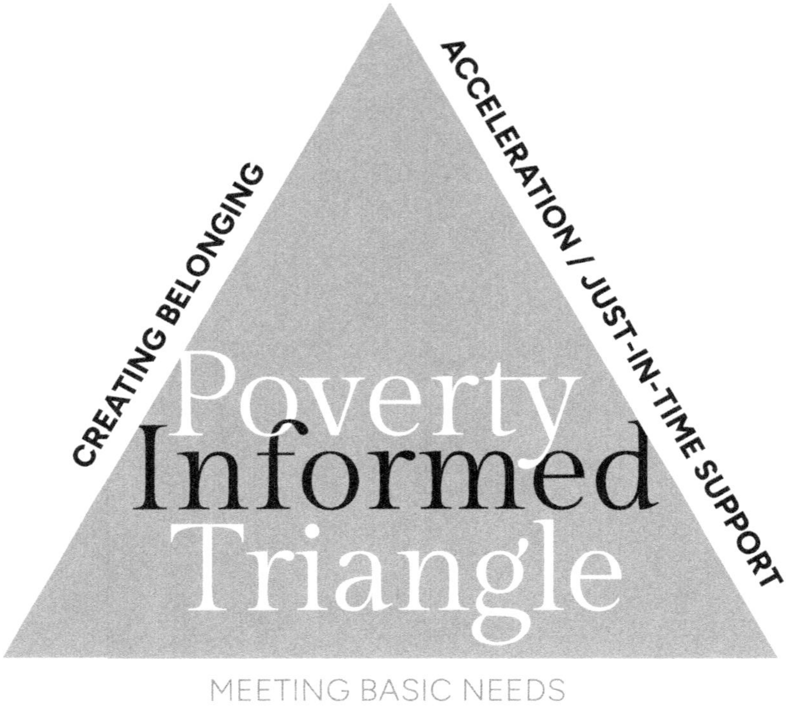
CREATING BELONGING
ACCELERATION / JUST-IN-TIME SUPPORT
Poverty
Informed
Triangle
MEETING BASIC NEEDS

7 Everyone Engages With Students

If you aspire to a poverty-informed approach that really gets different results, you don't have to be friends with people you serve, but I believe you do need to find a way to be in proximity to them and the truth of their stories. I believe you may have to take a risk and give up your safe distance to be more student facing. No one in your organization should have a position that never interacts with students. It is too dangerous and can allow students to become an abstraction. Poverty Informed Practice is truly centered on students. Even the business office can give tours or host a table at an open house.

EVERYONE ENGAGES WITH STUDENTS ⟶ THE POWER OF PROXIMITY

Anyone who has been in education has students who stick with them, some for a lifetime. Sarah is one of those students for me. I met Sarah while completing her high school equivalency diploma at the technical college where I was working. Sarah stood out, volunteering at her church and working with homeless people on a regular basis, including once hosting a Super Bowl party for a number of people with no place to go. She's pretty remarkable, but her path has not been easy. Sarah came to us from a few states away after living a life of poverty, poverty that forced her as a teenager to work in the carnival circuit to survive, poverty that showed in her speech and grammar that didn't align with our staff's middle class values. The kind of things that can make you forget to notice her brilliance.

Sarah came into my life at a time when I was working as a

school administrator and often separated from students. It was Sarah who decided I needed to get to know her, and I was blown away by the depth of her knowledge and the breadth of her interests. She would stop by my office to discuss something about school, and before I knew it, she would be helping me understand the challenges of living in a town where finding a reasonable place to live at a reasonable price is difficult. She is well versed in current events and has no shortage of opinions on how things can be improved. Sarah can be very direct and sometimes talks about things you wouldn't expect to talk about at school (she announced she was going to be an aunt in a way that made me blush), but she is direct, compassionate, and genuine. Poverty Informed Practice is to suspend judgment, and Sarah is a walking, breathing example of why we must. If we had written her off, we would have missed out on so much.

My friend Sarah reminds me that, no matter your school position, you need proximity to the people you serve, you need to be partners in their dreams. We are not searching for diamonds in the rough who can meet our expectations, we are trying to open our eyes and see the strengths students like Sarah bring to our college and the world. You LOVE them and all their outrageous humanity and raw courage. You eliminate the word enabling from your vocabulary, and you work to get people what they need. If you are lucky, you might make a friend like Sarah.

CHAPTER 5

POVERTY INFORMED PRACTICE

3 Actions to Deepen Systemic Change

ACCELERATION / JUST-IN-TIME SUPPORT
CREATING BELONGING
Poverty
Informed
Triangle
MEETING BASIC NEEDS

8 Every Barrier That Can Be Removed, Should Be Removed

"Empathy is getting down on your knees and looking at someone else in the eye, and realizing you could be them and all that separates you is luck."
- Dennis Lehane

REMOVING BARRIERS IN THE CLASSROOM ⟶ WE DON'T ALWAYS SEE THE FULL PICTURE

Sometimes there are words that just stop you in your tracks. I can't remember where I read it, but I was reading about one of my current heroes, Dr. Sara Goldrick-Rab, and her creation of the Faculty and Students Together (FAST) fund to grant emergency support to students with minimal red tape. I may be paraphrasing, but she said something along the lines of, "I don't spend any time worrying about who deserves this money, because lots of people deserve this money." It was the perfect way of describing the flaw in so much of what we do to help people. We waste incredible amounts of time trying to decide who deserves the help and put students in situations where they have to tell their story multiple times and hope to qualify for help when the criteria say they deserve it. Dr. Goldrick-Rab's simple statement punched a hole right in the middle of that kind of thinking and laid bare the implications and power differentials that are flaws in what is surely well intended. In response to this realization, a colleague and I worked with our Foundation

Director to establish a school FAST Fund that honors the faculty-student relationship. You can learn more about Dr. Goldrick-Rab's work here: http://saragoldrickrab.com/fastfund/ but that's not the story I want to tell.

This story is about how you have to keep challenging your basic assumptions throughout your career. If you don't, you can end up in well-intended places that are really just kind of wrong in hindsight. It's also a story about embedded practice and what becomes normal and the incredible resistance that can create change. As I move down the road of what we are calling Poverty Informed Practice, I encounter resistance in the oddest spots and over the smallest things. And it almost always has to do with the idea of who deserves something. Our driving statement is "Every barrier that CAN BE removed SHOULD BE removed," but getting there is an ongoing project.

EVERY BARRIER THAT CAN BE REMOVED SHOULD BE REMOVED.

One of the areas we administered was preparation and testing for the Certificate of General Educational Development (GED). It's a checkpoint on the way to college and changing economic reality for hundreds of our students every year. Classes are free, but there is a fee for testing and that can be a barrier. Ten years ago, I helped create a GED Assistance Fund that students could apply to if they needed help with costs so paying wouldn't be a barrier. And with the best of intentions, we built a process with criteria, we donated and fundraised, and our process culminated with the student meeting with the dean (that was me) finalizing the award. We asked if they had exhausted other options and evaluated where they were in their progress so we would be making a good investment. We were afraid we would run out of money, so criteria and screening seemed wise. Based on what I know now, I want to go back and shake me for the process I developed, but at the time it seemed well intentioned, and it would allow me to have contact with students in a personal way and help me stay connected to the day to day challenges they face. I even ran around campus touting the stories I heard, so people would understand the college experience for our most vulnerable students. Oh yeah, and I granted the funding to 100% of students who met with me.

Fast forward nine years, through a collection of amazing stories, and lots of successful students, and now I know I was dead wrong. The first hints were at faculty meetings when a couple brave faculty said they thought some students avoided applying because meeting with a dean was too intimidating, and they didn't want to have to tell their story again. "But how could that be?" I asked. "I love these conversations, and I think we really connect, and I grant the funding every time." I protested. It seemed clear the research said help plus a personal connection was the right thing to do, so I didn't listen and plowed on. I even created our FAST Fund which acknowledged the primacy of faculty to student relationships, but kept my own blind spot.

Later, I was bragging to two of my co-workers about FAST and how it was exactly what students needed and it respected the student. They looked at me incredulously and said, "Do you not see the contrast to GED Assistance?". And to be honest, I couldn't. I had created it, I was proud of it, and I was pretty sure the personal connection to students was important. My co-workers pushed back and said they were sure that connection was important, but couldn't we do that elsewhere and change the fund. I'd like to say a thunderbolt hit me, and I got it that day, but mostly I got mad. The afternoon conversation led to an evening of texting back and forth, and it's embarrassing to admit how entrenched I was in my old idea. All I could hear was I had done it wrong and that made me defensive. Eventually one of these trusted co-workers told me that my well-intentioned system was coercive, and that seemed to be the word that got my attention. We had set up a system to figure out who deserved help, when in reality, lots of people deserve help. We (I) had set up a system where a student had to tell and retell their story to get what they need, and we then encouraged/required them to write thank you notes to encourage more donors. It was coercive and that realization hurt.

So we stopped. We moved to a FAST type model but went even further. Any staff in our area who were aware of a student who needed funding can authorize it, no questions asked. In our field, relationships get built in lots of places, with faculty, with office staff, with counselors, and yes even with administrators. A student should only have to share their story one time, with someone they trust. Now we wonder what other systems that were built with the best of intentions could be much better and create that sense of belonging we are striving for? I wonder if readers will see similar flaws in their own work. There is so much to be done and figuring out who deserves help isn't relevant. Everyone needs help.

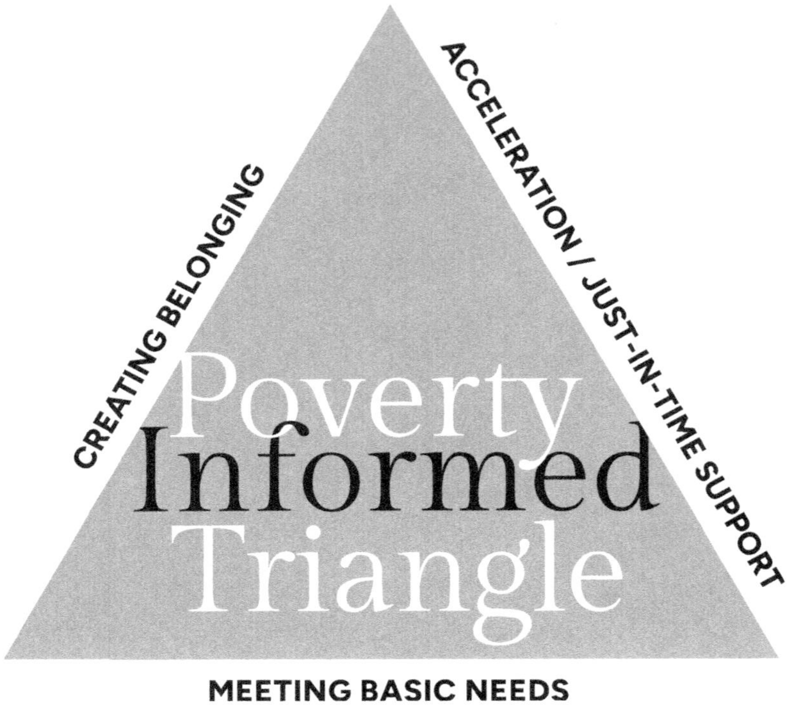
Poverty
Informed
Triangle
CREATING BELONGING
ACCELERATION / JUST-IN-TIME SUPPORT
MEETING BASIC NEEDS

9 Love Students More Than Policies

Our organizations are designed around lives and norms that do not match the lives and norms of our students in poverty. We can mitigate this systemic disadvantage by leaning toward the student every time a gray area in a policy gives us a chance to.

LOVE STUDENTS MORE THAN POLICIES ⟶ UNINTENDED CONSEQUENCES

Working as a newly appointed vice president of a community college, I learned I had a duty I was not aware of. It turns out if you run out of appeals to return from academic suspension, your last chance is to reach out to me. Roughly half a dozen students contacted me desperately seeking to return to school. Our current college policy was that you are on academic warning if your semester GPA is under a C or 2.0 average. The result is suspension for two consecutive semesters with the option to appeal to a committee. The appeal committee looks at the circumstances and tries to work on a plan for a successful return. Most appeals are granted, and the student returns with requirements they must meet. If they don't meet the requirements, the policy says they are suspended from school for a year with no opportunity to appeal. But there is a backdoor appeal (students are resourceful) and it involves reaching out to me. Thus, I had several to review before spring term, and I agonized over it. It brought up some memories from my past, and more so, it brought up concerns we weren't accomplishing what we meant to.

My personal memory is a story I had not thought about in a long time. Thirty some years ago, I had transferred colleges after three years. My experience at the first large big 10 college is a long story, but I left there with extraordinarily mixed results. I was academically eligible, but there were giant GPA swings and switching between part-time and full-time status. Instead of speaking to an advisor or someone from the college reaching out to me about my odd record, I just left, transferring schools to what I'd hoped would be a fresh start.

At my second college, I signed up for a full-time schedule, took a full-time job, and sincerely wanted to get my life in order. That's when my demons resurfaced. I didn't have a name for it back then, but mostly I was struggling with a pretty serious anxiety disorder. Unfortunately, in those days, I thought I was just a procrastinator and lazy. Whatever it was, after about six weeks, I stopped attending classes and went into avoidance and hiding, which was not a new behavior for me. Unsurprisingly, I got a 0.0 GPA for the term and over semester break I got a letter. It said due to my academic performance, I was suspended from the college for the next two semesters. I'm guessing the letter said other things, but I don't remember them,and that is the point. All I knew was I had failed, and I was in trouble.

I'm guessing the letter probably had an appeal process, but I was never going to do that. I was ashamed, and I would have done anything to hide the truth from people I loved. This means there were probably wonderful staff at the college just waiting for me to come in so they could help me get on track, and I'm sure the policy was intended to do just that. Realistically, I was never going to come in. It was that first brush with policy which started a series of events that defined most of the decade for me.

With my new suspension, I knew I needed to have a cover story. So, I quickly told my family I was unsure of my future, and I needed to take time off from school to get my plan straight. It was plausible and felt like it might buy me time. But you don't know what you don't know. I had student loans, and apparently you must start paying those six months after you drop out, who knew? I didn't have any money (I worked 3rd shift at a fast food restaurant), so I needed another plan. Being broke sometimes steals your ability to make decisions which make sense to others. It's part of the context of being in crisis.

My decision was to quickly enroll at a school up the road which was on a quarter system and could take me in March, staving off the student loan problem. Of course, I was still broke, and it would add miles to my commute, but between anxiety and financial difficulty the short-term decision was the one I made. I enrolled at the last minute, with no real financial plan and unsure how my suspension in one state impacted enrollment in another (this was pre-internet, I'm old), and this was obviously a recipe for failure. My term did not go well, but the policy at my new college said I was just on a warning. That meant a letter I could ignore. I felt like I'd dodged a bullet and enrolled for fall. And still, in three colleges, no one had reached out to me except with a letter. I'm sure the letter had all kinds of resources in it, but shame makes it easier to throw those things away and hope for a fresh start on Monday. Sort of like how some of us approach dieting.

Well, the next term at my third school didn't go well, and I received a one quarter suspension. I remember the letter said you could appeal or just sit out, so I sat out. And when I returned, I didn't make the standard again and this time the letter said you sit out a year. I vaguely recall some language about an appeal, but c'mon, was I really going to do that? After all my failures, now I would go ask for mercy? I was an intelligent guy, I had all the test scores to prove it, and here I sat in my shame and failures. I also grew up poor, and it made me defensive about asking for help. We blame poor people for being poor, and we celebrate boot strap stories about overcoming obstacles life has put in the way.

The combination of so many failures and a belief I should be able to do it on my own made it seem like seeking help was a weakness, and it was my job to fix issues caused by my deficits. My year suspension turned into three years before I returned. In between was in default on student loans and the destruction of my credit. The bright, talented 18-year-old returned to his third campus as an emotionally beat down 27-year-old. And that 27-year-old told himself when he was scared he would seek help, and sometimes I did, but even though my grades were good, it was still a struggle financially. I was certainly past believing anyone thought I might deserve extra help.

The spring of my 2nd year back, I was out of money and it was over. Maybe it was desperation, or maturity, or maybe my confidence had returned a little bit in the prior year, but for the first time I looked on campus for assistance. I went into the financial aid office and asked to speak to someone. It's hard to explain how ashamed and anxious I was. I still remember his name. It was Greg and he had a beard, that's all I remember. But he asked what I needed, and I said I was out of money and didn't know what to do. I'm getting teary-eyed writing this, but he didn't judge me for a second, and he told me about unsubsidized loans, and suddenly I had a lifeline. I didn't have to work 40 hours a week, I didn't have to quit. I didn't have to fail. I never told Greg, but he changed my life. I'm where I am today in large part because he was kind and solutions-oriented. I was a former loan defaulter, and I was 11 years from when I started college. I don't know what the policy said I deserved, but Greg saw me and gave me hope.

So, what's the point? The point is policy has impact, and it doesn't always match the intent. My colleges had policies of letters with wonderful information in them. And if I'd had the courage to read them, maybe I'd have shortened my education journey. I wonder how many students read those letters, no matter how well done. How could I know most appeals are granted? Who knows there is an appeal to the vice president not really spelled out in policy, but just in practice for those who know how to navigate the system? When I think about the half dozen students who came to me, I wonder how many didn't. Our policies are supposed to help, not punish. I don't think we design punitive policy on purpose, but I think being poverty-informed means we need to look at what we are doing very carefully.

No, I didn't let all of the students who came to me back into school immediately. I did speak to each of them in person or by phone, and if my decision was to delay their enrollment, I asked them to meet with me personally to make a plan. I'm not saying I did anything magic or even the right thing. I'm saying a poverty-informed college doesn't hide behind policy. We wrestle and agonize with these decisions because being a professional requires it. I'm not anti-policy, on the contrary, I'm advocating for understanding the power and implications of policy choices. I'm advocating for transparency and for policy with a student success focus at every turn. More than anything, I'm advocating for human connection in policy to normalize help and remove stigma from struggle. We all want better outcomes, that careful policy making and application provides.

LOVE STUDENTS MORE THAN POLICIES ⟶ STOP DOING THINGS THAT DON'T MAKE SENSE

"Some People Get Into the Habit of Being Loyal to a Mistake" -Richard Russo

"Stop doing things that don't make sense" may not sound intellectual, but it is really important. The most common story I share is about putting stickers on books. In past years, the division I led ordered a lot of workbooks for students, hundreds and even thousands. Every time we received a shipment of books, my office staff would spend hours putting stickers on the books reading "Property of _____. DO NOT Remove." This was usually a day or two of work for multiple people. In fact, it was often assigned as a project to someone who usually had other duties, but it was pointless. Our books were rarely stolen, and if they were, no one believed a warning sticker would prevent the theft. Worse yet, every student who came in was now reminded we thought they were potential thieves. Essentially, we had created a system that didn't work, took up time we did not have, to prevent something that was not occurring, and turned our students into suspects at the same time.

In the spirit of creating a sense of belonging through Poverty Informed Practice, I said we would no longer put stickers on books. In fact, we would remove the ones we had already put on there. Problem solved, right? If only it were that simple.

"But we put stickers on books Chad," was the first answer I received. So I shared my epiphany that it not only wasted time they did not have, did nothing, or worse yet, it did damage. "But we put stickers on books Chad, that is what we do." I was astounded, but Richard Russo wouldn't have been. We had not challenged this practice in anyone's memory, and now it was just standard operating practice. My objection seemed as odd to my staff as the practice now did to me. But I told them to stop anyway, and the problem was solved ... sure.

No. At first, they said let's just not do it with any new books, but leave the ones we have already done. It's a lot of work they said, and I almost agreed. Fortunately, a fellow Poverty Informed practitioner in another department suggested I have courage in my conviction and hold my ground. She reminded me, as she often does, people will work very hard to do new things the old way, and if I wanted to really shift what we were doing, this might be the place to start. So I did. I came back the next day and said we are going to remove stickers, and if I must do it myself, I will be glad to do so. It took another four months to get people to stop putting stickers on books. Being loyal to a mistake can be a habit indeed.

The sticker story is always a gateway for me to think about other things we do which do not make sense and work in opposition to our goal of fostering a sense of belonging. Things like trying to increase student success by suspending students who aren't succeeding. Almost every school I've worked with has a version of this policy. Surely, we can do better. As someone who lived through a suspension myself, there was not much I could do while they sent me away to fix myself. In fact, in those olden days, what I needed was someone to ask me, "why have your grades dropped so dramatically?" but no one ever did.

Decisions made a long time ago are not made sacred by age, and a decision they can make today likely has the same amount of wisdom attached to it. It is my way of saying do not grant loyalty to something just because it is how things have always been done. This has been a hard-earned lesson for me. I want to reach the place of how things should be permanently, but I doubt such a place exists. A Poverty Informed organization will seek the wisdom of the people it serves and will challenge its assumptions regularly. A Poverty Informed organization is a learning organization and will realize the current system generates exactly the results it was designed to generate. Look around your work spaces. Question the stamps, signs, and other images that tell students they are not welcome, and work to change it.

CREATING BELONGING
ACCELERATION / JUST-IN-TIME SUPPORT
Poverty
Informed
Triangle
MEETING BASIC NEEDS

10 Conduct a Fearless Self-Inventory for Bias

Poverty has been a life-long interest for me based on personal circumstance and experience. It has been a professional focus for the past 20 years after rereading Dr. Payne's A Framework for Understanding Poverty (Payne, R.K. 2005). I read the book in college about eight years earlier and I didn't see myself in it, but this time, I could see elements of my family's story in there. I know Dr. Payne has her critics (as we all do), but it was a great doorway into this octopus of an issue called poverty.

In the years after, I broadened my background and found other ways of looking at the issue, but I am grateful for that first experience and the new way of looking at the world. As educators, one of the best actions we can take to combat our poor student's learned helplessness and hopelessness is to take a heartfelt self-inventory of our own implicit bias. There are of course many ways to do this, one way is to use a ready made, researched based inventory located on page 112 in the back of this book. If you decide to do this exercise, remember there is no one looking over your shoulder to judge you. Respond honestly, and you may be surprised to uncover truths about your own bias or what you believe to be true that is in fact a well accepted myth.

ANALYZING RESULTS ⟶ HOW TO UNDO IMPLICIT BIASES

Any items you answer that do not correspond to the research-based conclusions could be indicative of hidden implicit bias. Implicit biases are unconscious beliefs, attitudes, or stereotypes, which influence our perceptions, words, and actions without our awareness (Kirwan Institute, 2016). Most implicit biases are learned over time, in families, schools, and communities. They come from the media, what we read, movies we watch, and listening to our friends talk. These are deep, unconscious beliefs that influence our actions and interpretations, and they are quite often inaccurate and may contradict our stated, conscious beliefs (Kirwan Institute, 2016). Implicit biases are often activated involuntarily, without an individual's awareness or intentional control. Fortunately, implicit biases can be unlearned (Godsil 2015).

Understanding what our biases are is the first step. Recognizing how they manifest in our thoughts and behavior is the second. Taking action to change our behavior is the third. Hard, but not complicated. One of the consequences of my own personal learning is I've discarded some insidious use of language I hear elsewhere all the time. I'd like to share a little about what I don't say anymore and why I think it matters for being poverty informed.

THINGS I DON'T SAY ANYMORE

Skin in the Game

This term gets tossed around easily at my workplace, and I'm sure many others. It's a glib way of saying people only value things they pay for. Looking at that phrase through a Poverty Informed view, you see just how judgmental it is. It is usually used to justify putting up some barrier for people before they can access help. It is based on an absolutely false assumption, and it implies that paying for something is the only way to be invested. What a privileged point of view. I would argue our students sacrifice endlessly to be a student all while managing complicated lives. Often, it can be an act of courage just to cross our threshold. Then we have the nerve to question their skin in the game. It is the height of arrogance and the opposite of Poverty Informed.

Common Sense

Common sense is another expression I haven't uttered in years other than to talk about it in training. Every time you hear this little gem, please think "common to whom?". In my experience, the declaration of common sense is a way of establishing in and out groups. To use Framework terminology (Payne, R. K. 2005), common sense is a set of hidden rules that exclude people and prevent them from success. I often hear the expression used when people don't behave the way we expect them to or when people violate our hidden rules which some believe are just common sense, and we often assume they aren't very smart or aren't ready yet.

Imagine for a moment, middle class, middle aged adults navigating our young students' lives for a week. Do you think our ignorance of their hidden rules might stick out, making us appear less capable and intelligent than we believe ourselves to be? Poverty informed practice begins with mutual respect, and part of that is understanding the myth of common sense.

Deserving

The last concept I have tried to dismiss as I've grown and learned is the concept of deserving. This is less a term I hear and more of an assumption that underlies so much of what we do for one another. In education, we spend substantial energy and resources trying to figure out who deserves our help, when in reality everyone needs help sometimes.

Consider Dr. Sara Goldrick-Rab and her creation of the Faculty and Students Together (FAST) fund to grant emergency support to students with as little red tape as possible (Goldrick-Rab, S., Hacker, N. L. et al 2021). The philosophy behind the FAST fund is to recognize that it's non-efficient to spend time worrying about who deserves assistance because such a large percentage of students need help.

Sadly, the idea of deserving is deep and shows up everywhere in agency time and so many other hurdles we put up to process and screen students. I've fallen victim to it myself, even with the best of intentions. A perception of scarcity drives this conversation, and it is not based in reality. We have plenty, why waste resources and effort defining some false line of who deserves help. Wouldn't you rather err on the side of helping?

REPLACE RESPECT AND RELATIONSHIP INTO DAILY VOCABULARY

Most of us, including myself, are about two bad breaks from needing financial assistance. When you start with that perspective and acknowledge your own luck and privilege, I doubt you will ever refer to "it's just common sense" again. When you remember the effort, courage, and yes sometimes heroism it takes for students from poverty to come to us and trust us, you won't ever talk about "skin in the game" again. And when you look behind well intended programs and see well intended machinery that simply sorts out who deserves and who doesn't, I hope you will build new structures that make help the default. I hope you will build systems founded on respect and relationships that honor our students. That is the vision of Poverty Informed practice.

CHAPTER 6

Final Words
OF ENCOURAGEMENT

Love Students to Success

Poverty Informed Practice is hard, but not complicated. In fact, it's so simple that most of the actions boil down to love. Love. Just typing that word makes my Midwestern, Scandinavian soul a little uneasy, because it seems a little out there. But, there it is. I hear the folks at Amarillo College talk about "loving the students you have" and it is powerful. I've heard Dr. Lowery-Hart and his team talk about loving their students to success, and it's an accurate description encapsulating what works.

As a Poverty Informed Practitioner, I know love is necessary for students to succeed, love that looks like becoming a partner in pursuit of student dreams, and working to remove system barriers getting in the way of those dreams as if they were my own.

It would certainly be easier to stay at a distance and not know, but if we are truly going to love the students we have, we need to dig in and see how we can help. Help, even though loving your students means you are going to suffer a little. Suffer a little, hearing and acknowledging every student's poverty truth which will compel you to give up the comfortable distance and privilege keeping you safe. Suffer a little frustration when bureaucracy combats you as it always does. Suffer upsetting people a little because this work will require upsetting people, and if you can't get comfortable with that, you might suffer a lot. In all honesty, it's my biggest challenge... I like to be liked.

When you love the students you have, you decide that readiness is signified by the audaciously courageous act of coming to us and telling us you want to go to school. If someone you loved told you they wanted that, how would you react? If you decide to love your students, shouldn't you react the same way?

Invitation to Get Started

As Poverty Informed practitioners, it is hard to know what to do with all of this and how and where to start. But, if after more than 20 years, someone like me still feels like a misfit, imagine what the person crossing your threshold must feel. Trust me, the people you serve who have been in the crisis of poverty already are questioning whether they belong in your spaces. It is now your job to show them they belong. What I invite you to do is this:

1. Welcome them exactly as they are.
2. Find value in who they are right now and not in who they will be when they learn to act like you.
3. Yes, they should be welcomed. More importantly, they need to know they are wanted. People in the crisis of poverty need to know your school is for people just like them.
4. You aren't going to fix them, per se, you are going to value them and lean into their strengths and gifts.
5. You aren't going to shake your head when they say things you think they shouldn't, you are just going to radically accept them and embrace their glorious humanity. Would you be surprised if they might be carrying a chip of their own? Let's see what we can do to not let it derail their dreams.

6. There is no need to grow up poor, like I did, to become skilled at Poverty Informed Practice. Follow the suggested framework, challenge yourself to dig deep while taking action to truly see your students, and you are already there!

Find Your Reason: Emmie's Story

If you want to take on hard truths, systems, processes, bureaucracy, and implicit bias, you better have reasons that keep you going. I admire the students we serve and personal connections with their stories keep me going. One example is my former student Emmie.

Emmie returned to community college after years of homelessness and with many difficult barriers including ongoing housing insecurity. Loving Emmie to success means we must deal with knowing her personal challenges while giving up the comfortable distance and privilege that keeps us safe. We must deal with the fact that success is rarely linear and even though students are doing well one day, they remain in a precarious situation. That knowledge makes us vulnerable and being vulnerable and human is part of loving students to success. But Emmie and students like her embody hope, and I think we owe it to our students to do whatever we can to shrink and remove those barriers.

Emmie, mentioned above, is a recently published poet, and I want to leave you with her poem "I am." It's worth a read on the days when the journey to real Poverty Informed Practice seems too far. We can't stop. Emmie deserves our best effort.

I Am
by Emmie Curran

I am a beautiful survivor, but sometimes I think
I am a failure.

I wonder where this next road will take me.

I see happiness in my heart, I want a life that is
not this.

I am a beautiful survivor, but sometimes I
pretend to be what people think I am.

I feel defeated each way I go, I touch the streets
I came from.

I worry that no one understands me, I cry for the
soul that I can't have.

I am a beautiful survivor, and I understand that
nothing can stop me.

I say what flows through the air, I dream the day
I can have my soul.

I try to be happy but fail, I am a beautiful
survivor.

POVERTY INFORMED PRACTICE

Resources

Glossary of Poverty Informed Practice Terms

AGENCY TIME

The time poor people spend trying to meet their basic needs by making social service or other agency related appointments, navigating to those appointments then filling out intake forms, engaging in interviews, writing essays and other tasks to prove poverty.

DEFICIT MODEL

Long standing belief in our culture that if you are poor, it is your fault.

GET COMFORTABLE BEING UNCOMFORTABLE

Poverty Informed Practice requires us to be uncomfortable at times, taking unpopular viewpoints or actions in order to advocate and take action to support impoverished children.

GET OVER YOURSELF

Letting go of our pet project or of being recognized as THE reason someone else succeeds. It also means to stop defining success for people in poverty by seeing how much closer they are to acting like us. There is nothing magical about middle class values, they are just the dominant values.

IMPLICIT POVERTY BIAS

False, yet widely accepted views about people who are poor. Ideas about poverty that impact our thoughts, beliefs, and actions to unknowingly hurt students.

IT'S HARD BUT NOT COMPLICATED

Refers to the idea that being a Poverty Informed Practitioner is definitely challenging work, but at the same time the actions to take are straightforward and easy to grasp.

I SEE YOU

"I see you," is a South African Zulu greeting made popular in the epic film Avatar. It says, in essence, I see all of you, your light and your darkness, and I am always here for you with respect and love.

POVERTY INFORMED TRIANGLE

Includes the three fundamentals of Poverty Informed Practice: meeting basic needs, creating a sense of belonging, and supporting people just when they need it to accelerate their progress.

WHOLE SYSTEM IS RIGGED

Systems are set up to exploit the poverty of individuals. This includes bank fees, payday lending, exorbitant housing costs paired with lack of public housing.

Self Assessment

Ask yourself: What is a way that you are growing?

MINDSET

Consider these two different ways of thinking:

- Fixed mindset: Some people believe they either have what it takes to succeed or they don't. They think everything is pretty much settled and fixed. They have a fixed mindset.

  When stuff happens, they know they (or other people) are this or that kind of person, and the way things are is pretty much the way things will be. It's as if they are riding in a train, and they can only go where the tracks go.

- Growth mindset: Some people think that when things are going smoothly, or changing fast, or when things seem to be stuck, we have choices. We might need help seeing the choices that are available to us, but we can work to make things better. These people have a growth mindset.

  When things go wrong, they think about what they can say or do to make things go more the way they want them to go. It's as if they are riding a bike, and they can pedal faster or slower, turn left or right, or get the tire fixed if they have a flat.

WHICH MINDSET DO YOU HAVE? TEST YOURSELF!

Answer the following questions to offer clues as to your mindset. This is just for you & your own self-knowledge. There are no right or wrong answers:

1. People are either born with talent and intelligence or they're not, and you can't change how talented or intelligent you are.

Strongly agree Agree Disagree Strongly disagree

2. No matter who you are, you can develop your talent and intelligence all your life.

Strongly agree Agree Disagree Strongly disagree

3. Failing at something proves you do not have the talent or intelligence to succeed in it.

Strongly agree Agree Disagree Strongly disagree

4. The most important factor in success is effort—how hard and persistently a person works at something.

Strongly agree Agree Disagree Strongly disagree

Self-Inventory for Implicit Poverty Bias

COMMON BELIEFS ABOUT POVERTY

Below is a list of six statements that reflect common implicit bias about children and families living in poverty. Please rate your agreement with these statements, using a scale of 1–4 (1 = not at all, 2 = a little, 3 = often, and 4 = absolutely). Following this list are the research-supported conclusions, based on Reaching and Teaching Students in Poverty: Strategies for Erasing the Opportunity Gap (Gorski, 2013).

Common beliefs about poverty:

1. Children who grow up in poverty communicate poorly and use informal or non-standard English.

1 = not at all   2 = a little   3 = often   4 = absolutely

2. Low-income parents value education less than middle-class parents.

1 = not at all   2 = a little   3 = often   4 = absolutely

3. Parents living in poverty are attentive and involved in their children's lives.

1 = not at all   2 = a little   3 = often   4 = absolutely

4. Children who grow up in poverty have parents who are hardworking and resourceful.

1 = not at all   2 = a little   3 = often   4 = absolutely

5. Children who grow up in poverty are more likely to have parents or family members who are abusing drugs or alcohol.

1 = not at all   2 = a little   3 = often   4 = absolutely

6. Parents in poor families have goals and aspirations for their children.

1 = not at all   2 = a little   3 = often   4 = absolutely

COMMON BELIEF ANSWERS

Research supported (Gorski 2013):

1. **1 or 2** *Explanation:* Every language is rich and full of nuances used to communicate with complexity. The notion that a standard or formal version of English is somehow richer and more complex serves to limit expectations for students not coming from white, middle-class backgrounds. Low-income parents value education less than middle-class parents.

2. **1 or 2** *Explanation:* Low-income parents value education just as much as middle class parents. They know how important it is for their children. They may not be able to participate in school, due to a variety of factors.

3. **3 or 4** *Explanation:* Low-income parents are attentive and involved in their children's lives. They are as attentive as parents in other social classes.

4. **3 or 4** *Explanation:* Families in poverty work as hard, and sometimes harder, than their middle-class counterparts and are often working multiple jobs for longer hours and for lower wages.

5. **1 or 2** *Explanation:* The incidents of alcoholism are actually higher in wealthier families. Incidents of drug use and abuse are similar across socio-economic groups, but the types of substances used may vary. Those living in poverty have less access to medical care and intervention.

6. **3 or 4** *Explanation:* Poverty-level families have goals and aspirations for their children. They may not have the resources to make those goals come true, or know how to access resources for their children. When provided information about resources and programs, they actively pursue them.

Source:
Self Inventory Source: (Gibson, E.L. & Barr, R.D., 2017).

Can also be found on the U.S. Department of Education's website: https://files.eric.ed.gov/fulltext/EJ1275655.pdf

POVERTY
INFORMED PRACTICE

Group Activities

1 M&M Chain Stories

Action 4: Acknowledge the Truth
Action 10: Conduct a Fearless Self-Inventory for Bias

LEARNING TARGET

I can describe three ways someone living with poverty has system-based disadvantages as opposed to disadvantages due to personal flaws.

PREP

Treat size bag of M&M's enough for each student or staff member. Yes, this is an activity you can do with staff or students.

STEP ONE ⟶ SORT THE CANDY

Have students spread out in the classroom as comfortable. Instruct them to sort candy in any way they'd like to accept by color.

STEP TWO ⟶ MAKE A CHAIN STORY

Explain they are going to create a chain story with M&Ms as a theme. Chain stories start with a stem sentence which you, the leader, will provide. For example: "A funny thing happened on the way here today..." and then they pick up and continue one sentence or phrase at a time. Participants typically have fun during this part. Let them play creating sentences for a few minutes before changing the rules.

STEP THREE ⟶ ADDING NO 'M' OR 'N' RULE

Stop activity, and explain your omnipotent powers have eliminated the letters M and N from existence. Participants continue, and they have to either avoid those words or mispronounce them. They find this harder of course, and the story slows and struggles.

REFLECTION

Relieve their agony ending the game to reflect on what they noticed. Point out they didn't lose any intelligence in the 2nd scenario. They were just as talented and bright as they were before, but a lack of key resources took that appearance away. How do people judge those missing resources? Tie in facts vs. common implicit bias about poverty to deepen reflection.

MODIFY

Change up the reflection questions to cater to audience age, positions, current educational climate or goals, etc.

ACCOMMODATE

Add option to partner up to make chain stories to better support any neurodiverse students.

2 Three Question Interview

Action 4: Acknowledge the Truth
Action 7: Everyone Engages With Students

LEARNING TARGET

I can name three facts about one person in the room.

PREP

1. Arrange circle seating
2. Assign seats in the circle
3. Assign partners
4. Choose questions for the interview. Post on board/slide.

PARTNER GREETING

Students greet their assigned partners they will interview. Set up the greeting expectation by kinesthetically modeling for the group. "Hello, Robin." Robin responds, "Hello, Francis."

Review basics of a friendly and respectful greeting:

1. Sincere tone and body language.
2. Correctly pronounce name. If you don't know, ask!

To save time, partners greeting can be done with a student next to them in their assigned seat. Be specific about partnering students to avoid choosing friends.

STEP ONE
⟶ MODEL THE INTERVIEW

Use a kinesthetic model of the Three Question Interview to set interview expectations in a similar way you modeled the greeting. List the questions students may choose from for the interview.

The three questions:

1. "What foods do you enjoy? Why?"
2. "What do you like to do in your free time? Why?"
3. "What music do you like to listen to? Why?"

STEP TWO
⟶ INTERVIEWS BEGIN

Remind students to switch partners halfway through the allotted time frame to ensure balanced sharing/listening.

STEP THREE
⟶ PARTNER INTRODUCTIONS

Students take turns introducing their partner to the whole class. Remind students to listen carefully as they will be asked questions later about what they learned. Teachers write down one fact about each student to use for "who remembers."

REFLECTION

Who remembers? After everyone has shared information with the group, ask students to recall peoples' answers: "Who remembers what Alex likes to do?" "Who remembers Hayden's favorite game?" "Who in our group loves playing the piano?"

MODIFY

- Provide added structure by pre-choosing questions from the Friendly Share Topics (see below) or allow students to generate their own list of Friendly Share Topics.
- When doing activity with adults or in groups where a high level of trust is intact, questions can be of a more personal nature, but always with the option to pass on any question.

ACCOMMODATE

- For neurodiverse students who find recalling information or speaking in front of the group challenging, have them share only the interviewee's name or name and one thing about them.
- Allow students to use notecards or a device to record answers to share.

FRIENDLY SHARE TOPICS

- Share about a time when you were brave.
- What is the best gift you ever gave to someone? To whom did you give it?
- Describe the qualities of a good friend.
- Name something that stresses you in life and tell how you handle it.
- Describe the kind of person you would like to be when you are an adult.
- What is your favorite season, and why do you like it?
- What do you do to stay healthy?
- If you could eat only one food for the rest of your life, what would it be?
- Share the last random act of kindness you did.

- If you had $1,000,000 and had to give it all away in one day to someone you didn't know, how would you do so?
- Whom do you admire? Why?
- Share a family ritual.
- Describe the best day of your life. Describe your most successful class.
- If you could eliminate one emotion from your life, which would it be? Why?
- What was your favorite birthday so far? What made it special?
- What rule is most important in your home?
- What occupation (job) do you most admire?
- Describe a perfect day for you.
- What is your favorite holiday? How do you celebrate it?
- What is the best meal you ever had? Who made it?
- What scares you? Why?
- Tell what you would do differently if you were a parent. If you already are a parent, what do you do differently?
- Do you have a pet peeve? If so, what is it?
- How do you repair a relationship when you break it?
- Have you ever had a serious injury or illness? What was it, how did it happen, and what was the cure?

Source: Adapted with permission from High School Advisory Book, The Origins Program 2023. https://originsonline.org/

3 What Moves You

Action 2: Give Voice to Lived Experience

LEARNING TARGET

I can identify 3 differences between others' lived experiences and my own.

PREP

1. Arrange room so there is space for lining up and walking
2. Prepare statements to read or use ones provided

Note: This activity is best done with adults or with teenagers where there is a high level of comfort and trust. Always give an option to sit out if uncomfortable.

STEP ONE ⟶ EXPLAIN THE ACTIVITY

Players will line up on one end of the room. Statements will be read. As each statement is read, if the statement is true for you, take a step forward.

STEP TWO ⟶ READ STATEMENTS

Once students are lined up, begin to read statements. Customize statements to your group's age, maturity, etc. and be sure to give an option to skip if uncomfortable.

Here are a few thoughts for group activity 3. People should

answer these questions based on their youth:

1. If someone in your family was incarcerated, please take 3 steps back.
2. If you attended private school, take two steps forward.
3. If you recall not asking your parents for things other kids had because you didn't want to stress them out, take 1 step back.
4. If you recall going on vacation more than once in your youth, take 1 step forward.
5. If your family relied on assistance to stay food secure, take 2 steps back.
6. If you had your own room all through childhood, take 1 step forward.
7. If you lived in a home that has since been demolished, take 1 step back.
8. If you knew people in your immediate family who retired on more than social security, take a step forward.
9. If someone helped you pay for college take 2 steps forward.
10. If you were ever evicted take 3 steps back.

Note: Groups could devise other class related questions to spread people around the room. This illustrates that we do not all start from the same place.

REFLECTION

1. How could these circumstances change your worldview, your actions, your choices?
2. How do we create equity in these circumstances?
3. Are their universal solutions that would benefit all and at worst harm no one?
4. How did you feel during and after this exercise?

POVERTY INFORMED PRACTICE

Action Plans

1 Declaring the Movement

STAFF/DEPARTMENT RESPONSIBLE

DATE TO BEGIN

DUE DATE

RESOURCES REQUIRED

CHALLENGES ANTICIPATED

OUTCOME

2 Give Voice to Lived Experience

STAFF/DEPARTMENT RESPONSIBLE

DATE TO BEGIN

DUE DATE

RESOURCES REQUIRED

CHALLENGES ANTICIPATED

OUTCOME

3 Always Leave a Path Back

STAFF/DEPARTMENT RESPONSIBLE

DATE TO BEGIN

DUE DATE

RESOURCES REQUIRED

CHALLENGES ANTICIPATED

OUTCOME

4 Acknowledge the Truth

STAFF/DEPARTMENT RESPONSIBLE

DATE TO BEGIN

DUE DATE

RESOURCES REQUIRED

CHALLENGES ANTICIPATED

OUTCOME

5 Have a Bias for Action

STAFF/DEPARTMENT RESPONSIBLE

DATE TO BEGIN

DUE DATE

RESOURCES REQUIRED

CHALLENGES ANTICIPATED

OUTCOME

6 Practice Radical Hospitality

STAFF/DEPARTMENT RESPONSIBLE

DATE TO BEGIN

DUE DATE

RESOURCES REQUIRED

CHALLENGES ANTICIPATED

OUTCOME

7 Everyone Engages With Students

STAFF/DEPARTMENT RESPONSIBLE

DATE TO BEGIN

DUE DATE

RESOURCES REQUIRED

CHALLENGES ANTICIPATED

OUTCOME

8 Every Barrier That Can Be Removed, Should Be Removed

STAFF/DEPARTMENT RESPONSIBLE

DATE TO BEGIN

DUE DATE

RESOURCES REQUIRED

CHALLENGES ANTICIPATED

OUTCOME

9 Love Students More Than Policies

STAFF/DEPARTMENT RESPONSIBLE

DATE TO BEGIN

DUE DATE

RESOURCES REQUIRED

CHALLENGES ANTICIPATED

OUTCOME

10 Conduct a Fearless Self-Inventory for Bias

STAFF/DEPARTMENT RESPONSIBLE

DATE TO BEGIN

DUE DATE

RESOURCES REQUIRED

CHALLENGES ANTICIPATED

OUTCOME

DISCUSSION QUESTIONS

Book Study Guide

Discussion Questions

1. Dull argues that deficit model thinking, which stems from the belief that poverty is an individual character flaw problem, keeps our work focused on the individual, rather than the systemic barriers that create and perpetuate poverty. Do you agree with Dull? How many students in your school fall below the federal government's low income threshold? Is the emphasis of support on working to improve the system or the individuals?

2. Dull contends that poverty is often a no win situation and under continuous scrutiny. For example, if a student on food assistance has a shopping cart filled with treats, they would be accused of eating junk on their dime, but if they stocked up with fresh produce and other higher priced foods, they would hear comments about how it must be nice to have the government pay for food others can't afford. Based on your own observations, do you agree with Dull? (4). What other ways do you see poverty as a no win situation in the public eye? In what ways does your school help or hurt its impoverished families no win circumstance?

3. Dull notes "All too often we define 'success' for people in poverty by seeing how much closer they are to acting like us. There is nothing magical about middle class values, they are just the dominant values. We need to get over ourselves, see the strengths in the people we serve, and aid them in building on those strengths in ways that work for them, not necessarily what reflects us." (6) In what ways does your school expect poor

people to express middle class values? (7) Name some strengths of impoverished students you've worked with that are NOT reflective of middle class values.

4. The three sides of the Poverty Informed Triangle are: meeting basic needs, belonging and just in time support. What do you think is the most important side? Why? What do you think is the easiest side to address in the classroom? The most difficult?

5. Dull asserts that being a poverty informed practitioner is "hard, but not complicated." What do you think he means? Do you agree? Why or why not?

6. Declare a Movement is the first action step of a Poverty Informed Practitioner. Dull suggests a deliberate, unapologetic approach to tackle the crisis of poverty because "a watered down approach will give watered down results." What are some ways to Declare a Movement?

7. Action two, Giving Voice to Lived Experience, includes asking the magic question: What do you need to succeed? What are some ways this question could be asked within a classroom context? How about campus wide context?

8. Dull tells the story about his dad in action three, Always Leave a Path Back. Does your school allow for another chance, not just a second chance? What are some examples? How could this practice be enhanced?

9. In action four, Acknowledge the Truth, Dull challenges readers by asking: What will you do to say "I see you" to students? What is your response to this question?

10. The fifth action, Have a Bias for Action, requires us to remove the guilt of intervening on behalf of students who have nothing. Discuss some ways teachers may feel they are helping too much or too little.

11. To what extent, if any, does your school district or campus implement the sixth action of Radical Hospitality? How could your school community benefit from using similar intervention approaches?

12. What do you consider to be the pros and cons of the seventh action Everyone Engages with Students?

13. Every Barrier that Can be Removed, Should be Removed is the eighth action. What changes would have to be implemented where you work for this to happen?

14. For the ninth action, Love Students More Than Policies, Dull tells the story of his own college journey which included objective failures and internal struggles. Discuss Dull's story and any insights gained from it as it relates to Poverty Informed Practice.

15. Take the tenth action, Conduct a Fearless Self-Inventory for Bias. Share only as comfortable. Discuss whether there are any bias patterns among your group. If so, why do you think that is?

16. In his final words of encouragement, Dull states there is no need to grow up poor, like he did, to become skilled at Poverty Informed Practice. If you follow the suggested framework, challenge yourself to dig deep while taking action to truly see your students, then you are already there. What are some examples of how you are already there when it comes to Poverty Informed Practice? What would you like to take action on next?

POVERTY
INFORMED PRACTICE

References

Baker-Smith, C., Coca, V., Goldrick-Rab, S., Looker, E., Richardson, B., & Williams, T. (2020). #RealCollege 2020: Five years of evidence on campus basic needs insecurity. *The Hope Center.* https://tacc.org/sites/default/files/documents/2020-02/2019_realcollege_survey_report.pdf.

Beegle, D. M. (2000). Interrupting generational poverty: Experiences affecting successful completion of a bachelor's degree. *Portland State University.* http://doi.org/10.15760/etd.5709.

Beegle, D. M. (2003). Overcoming the silence of generational poverty. *Talking Points*, 15(1), 11-20. https://www.hawaii.hawaii.edu/sites/default/files/assets/kauhale-day/docs/overcoming-the-silence-of-generational-povertypdf.

Beegle, D. M., Ellis, D., & Akkary, R. (2007). *See poverty--be the difference!: Discovering the missing pieces for helping people move out of poverty.* Communication Across Barriers, Inc.

Bombardieri, M. (May 30, 2018). Colleges are no match for American poverty. *The Atlantic.* https://www.theatlantic.com/education/archive/2018/05/college-poor-students/560972/.

Bouchard, M., Denault, A. S., & Guay, F. (2023). Extracurricular activities and adjustment among students at disadvantaged high schools: The mediating role of peer relatedness and school belonging. *Journal of Adolescence.* https://doi.org/10.1002/jad.12132.

Castro, A. C. (2021). *How anticipated stigma and cultural mismatch impact first-generation college students' achievement: Exploring the mediating roles of psychological distress and sense of belonging* (Publication NO. 8548452) [Doctoral Thesis, California State University, Long Beach]. Proquest Dissertation Publishing.

Desmond, M. (2016). *Evicted: Poverty and profit in the American city*. Crown Publishers/Random House.

Desmond, M. (2023). *Poverty by America*. Crown Publishers/Random House.

Education Pays. (2022) *Career Outlook*. U.S. Bureau of Labor Statistics. https://www.bls.gov/careeroutlook/2023/data-on-display/education-pays.htm.

Freie, C. (2022). The Work and Activism of Sara Goldrick-Rab. *Taylor & Francis Group*. https://saragoldrickrab.com/wp-content/uploads/2023/07/The_Future_of_American_Higher_Education_How_Today..._-_12_Realcollege_theWork_and_Activism_of_Sara_Goldrick-Rab.pdf.

Freudenberg, N., Goldrick-Rab, S., & Poppendieck, J. (2019). College students and SNAP: The new face of food insecurity in the United States. *American Journal of Public Health*, 109(12), 1652-1658. https://doi.org/10.2105/ajph.2019.305332.

Gibson, E.L., & Barr, R.D., (2017). Building a culture of hop: Exploring implicit bias against poverty. *National Youth-At-Risk Journal*, 2 (2). https:doi.org/10.20429/nyarj.2017.020203.

Godsil, R. D. (2015). Breaking the cycle: Implicit bias, racial anxiety, and stereotype threat. *Poverty & Race*, 24(1), 1–2, 8–10. https://www.prrac.org/newsletters/janfeb2015.pdf.

Goldrick-Rab, S., & Cady, C. (2018). Supporting community college completion with a culture of caring: A case study of Amarillo College. *Temple university and Wisconsin HOPE Lab*. https://www.actx.edu/president/files/filecabinet/folder10/Wisconsin_HOPE_Lab___A_Case_Study_of_Amarillo_College__print_version_.pdf

Goldrick-Rab, S., Kelchen, R., Harris, D. N., & Benson, J. (2016). Reducing income inequality in educational attainment: Experimental evidence on the impact of financial aid on college completion. *American Journal of Sociology*, 121(6), 1762-1817. https://doi.org/10.1086/685442.

Goldrick-Rab, S., Hacker, N. L., Kienzl, G., Price, D. V., & Curtis, D. (2021). When Care Isn't Enough: Scaling Emergency Aid during the Pandemic. *Hope Center for College, Community, and Justice.*

Gorski, P. (2013). *Reaching and teaching students in poverty: Strategies for erasing the opportunity gap*. Teachers College Press.

Hagedorn-Hatfield, R.L., Hood, L. B. & Hege, A. (2022). A decade of college student hunger: What we know and where we need to go. *Front Public Health, 10.* https:doi.org/10.3389/fpubh.2022.837724.

Jaggars, S. S., & Stacey, G. W. (2014). What we know about developmental education outcomes. *Columbia University, Community College Research Center.* https://ccrc.tc.columbia.edu/media/k2/attachments/what-we-know-about-developmental-education-outcomes.pdf.

Maslow, A., & Lewis, K. J. (1987). Maslow's hierarchy of needs. *Salenger Incorporated*, 14(17), 987-990.

Kelly, A. P., & Goldrick-Rab, S. (2014). *Reinventing Financial Aid: Charting a New Course to College Affordability*. Harvard Education Press.

Lowery-Hart, R. (2022). Leading culture change: Moving from transformational initiatives to a transformational institution. *Change: The Magazine of Higher Learning*, 54(3), 5-10. https://doi.org/10.1080/00091383.2022.2054172

Lowery-Hart, R., & Pacheco, G. (2011). Understanding the first-generation student experience in higher education through a relational dialectic perspective. *New Directions for Teaching and Learning*, 2011 (127), 55-68. https://doi.org/10.1002/tl.457.

Martin, G., & Ardoin, S. (2023). *Social class supports: Programs and practices to serve and sustain poor and working-class students through higher education.* Taylor & Francis.

Ornish, D., & Ornish, A. (2022). *Undo it!: How simple lifestyle changes can reverse most chronic diseases.* Ballantine Books.

Payne, R. (1996). Understanding and working with students and adults from poverty. *Instructional Leader*, 9(2), 1-5.

Payne, Ruby K. "A framework for understanding poverty." (2005).

Savoie-Roskos, M., Hood, L., Hagedorn-Hatfield, R., Landry, M., Patton-López, M., Richards, R., Mann, G. (2023). Creating a culture that supports food security and health equity at higher education institutions. Public Health Nutrition, 26(3), 503-509. https://10.1017/S1368980022002294

Shaw, K. M., Goldrick-Rab, S., Mazzeo, C., & Jacobs, J. A. (2006). *Putting poor people to work: How the work-first idea eroded college access for the poor.* Russell Sage Foundation.

Sobey, F., & Lowery-Hart, R. (2022). You Want to Close Equity Gaps? Embrace 100% Co-Requisite Approach to Developmental Education. *Recognizing Promise: The Role of Community Colleges in a Post Pandemic World* (69-80). Emerald Publishing Limited.

Statts, C. (2016). Understanding implicit bias. *America Educator, winter 2015-2016*. https://files.eric.ed.gov/fulltext/EJ1086492.pdf.

Turnbull, K. L., Mateus, D. M. C., LoCasale-Crouch, J., Coolman, F. L., Hirt, S. E., & Okezie, E. (2022). Family routines and practices that support the school readiness of young children living in poverty. *Early Childhood Research Quarterly, 58*, 1-13.

Van Canegem, T., Van Houtte, M., & Demanet, J. (2022). Grade retention: A pathway to solitude? A cross-national multilevel analysis of the effects of being retained on students' sense of belonging. *Comparative Education Review*, 66(4), 664-687.

Williams, C. L., Hirschi, Q., Sublett, K. V., Hulleman, C. S., & Wilson, T. D. (2020). A brief social belonging intervention improves academic outcomes for minoritized high school students. *Motivation Science,* 6(4), 423–437. https://doi.org/10.1037/mot0000175.

Yeh, C. T., & Wodtke, G. T. (2023). The effects of head start on low-Income mothers. *Socius*, 9, https://doi.org/10.1177/237802312311923.

About the Author

Chad Dull, Ed.D., is an award-winning educator with 30 years of experience as a classroom teacher, college faculty, staff development instructor, college administrator, and public speaker.

In his 20s, he spent time as a daycare aide and teacher, serving people at a wide range of income levels, while living in poverty himself as did most of his co-workers. He also spent four years chasing a dream of being a college basketball coach, but forgot to graduate from college. Then he did what a lot of former poor kids do, became a teacher and spent time seeing what elementary schools looked like through the lens of poverty. He was also a high school basketball coach, spending time with kids of all ages before moving onto the two-year college sector, where he spent the next two decades as an instructor, grant coordinator, associate dean, dean, and finally vice president.

Currently, Dr. Dull works in a K-12 public school district as a Community Impact Coordinator in close proximity to people living the challenges of the crisis of poverty every day. He also is a popular keynote speaker, blogger and professional development presenter. Audiences everywhere respond to his use of humor and sensitivity to remind them of how important educators are in the lives of students. His insights about Poverty Informed Practice in Education are extraordinary. Through research-based theory, poignant stories, and hilarious characterizations, he connects with the souls of all who are involved in education.

Dr. Dull can be reached through his website:
povertyinformedpractice.com

Printed in Great Britain
by Amazon

43402980R00096